# KEEPING
# YOUR BALANCE

GOSPEL
ADVOCATE
A TRUSTED NAME SINCE 1855

Gospel Advocate Company
P.O. Box 150
Nashville, Tennessee 37202

# KEEPING
# YOUR BALANCE

## Nancy Eichman

# OTHER BOOKS BY NANCY EICHMAN

*God's Makeover Plan*

*Seasoning Your Words*

Published by Gospel Advocate Co.
P.O. Box 150, Nashville, TN 37202
http://www.gospeladvocate.com

ISBN: 0-89225-472-6

# DEDICATION

With much love – To two special ladies who have
balanced many things in their lives:

My mother Milbra Spivey Chaffin

My mother-in-law Zelmodene Callicoat Eichman

# ACKNOWLEDGEMENTS

Thanks again, dear friends and family –

Jane McWhorter, Connie Pyles and Phil Eichman
for your assistance with the manuscript.

Phil, John and Amy Eichman
for your love and support.

# TABLE OF CONTENTS

Page

Preface . . . . . . . . . . . . . . . . . . . . . . . . . . . . . . . . . . . . . . . .9

1  Beyond the Rat Race . . . . . . . . . . . . . . . . . . . . . . . . . . . . .11

2  Overwhelmed . . . . . . . . . . . . . . . . . . . . . . . . . . . . . . . .19

3  Choosing the Better Part . . . . . . . . . . . . . . . . . . . . . . .27

4  Rocks in Your Jar . . . . . . . . . . . . . . . . . . . . . . . . . . . . . .35

5  How Crazy Is Your Quilt? . . . . . . . . . . . . . . . . . . . . . . .43

6  Time Matters . . . . . . . . . . . . . . . . . . . . . . . . . . . . . . . .51

7  Save, Scrimp or Squander? . . . . . . . . . . . . . . . . . . . . . .61

8  Stuffing Your Stuff . . . . . . . . . . . . . . . . . . . . . . . . . . . .69

9  Giving Your Gifts Back . . . . . . . . . . . . . . . . . . . . . . . . .79

10  Running on Empty . . . . . . . . . . . . . . . . . . . . . . . . . . . .87

11  Meeting Your Best Friend . . . . . . . . . . . . . . . . . . . . . . .95

12  Relating to Your Relatives . . . . . . . . . . . . . . . . . . . . .103

13  They'll Know We Are Christians . . . . . . . . . . . . . . . . . .111

Endnotes . . . . . . . . . . . . . . . . . . . . . . . . . . . . . . . . . . .121

# IN BALANCE OR IMBALANCED?

Are you in balance or imbalanced? It has been said that one out of four Americans is imbalanced. Think of your three closest friends. If they are okay, you are in trouble!

Probably we have all felt out of balance at one time or another. Perhaps it is a constant, pervading, sinking feeling of being overwhelmed. Maybe it just strikes when a family member is sick at the same time the plumbing is stopped up and a deadline is due. Balance is that illusive even keel in the midst of life's uproar. It is a constant search for the happy medium, the peaceful middle ground in a world of extremes.

The world has many solutions to our out-of-sync lives, but ultimately none of them will work. No organizational system can really put our lives together. No book about time or money management can totally save us. No to-do list can truly tell us what we must do. No planner can give us real direction. We need to look beyond our overcrowded schedules and misplaced priorities to see Christ as the focus of our lives.

That's what this book is about – looking to Jesus who grew in perfect balance.

By understanding how our Lord lived a well-rounded life – mentally, physically, spiritually and socially – we can better find an equilibrium for our own. We hope to explore some balance busters like guilt, procrastination and perfectionism. By examining God's

Word, we will look at how we can better balance the use of our time, money, possessions and talents. We can learn how to set priorities to strengthen our relationships with our families, other Christians, friends, work associates, and most importantly, our heavenly Father.

To further your personal study and class discussion, each chapter concludes with "Balance Check," 10 questions that delve further into each chapter's topic, and "Time Out," a collection of quotes from various sources pertinent to the subject of the chapter.

## CHAPTER 1

# BEYOND THE RAT RACE

*"The trouble with the rat race is that even
if you win you're still a rat." – Lily Tomlin[1]*

D o you sometimes feel like a rat in the rat race of life? Do you feel like you are wandering through a maze with no particular direction? How many mornings do you feel like you are starting another day as a marathon runner? How many evenings have you landed in a frazzled heap of exhaustion and wondered where the day went?

Even if we try to be efficient, sometimes it seems that no amount of organization can help us accomplish all we need to do. With so many expectations and demands wearing on us, we feel stretched to the limit. We fritter away the hours of our lives by meeting the immediate demands. We wonder if our activity accomplishes anything important. We feel like rats, running frantically and going nowhere fast. We long for balance, a feeling that the activities of our lives are fitting together in proportion, harmony and purpose. Instead, we often feel imbalanced and out of sync with our surroundings and with God.

This is especially disheartening to Christian women because we think we should be the epitome of balance. While the world struggles with juggling time, money, family and more, we should be able to manage it all nicely, right? Unfortunately, we often suf-

fer the same fallout from imbalance: stress, guilt, worry, worka-
holism and strained family relations.

## WE BALANCE MANY ROLES

In life we assume many roles. Some roles we eagerly accept;
others are thrust upon us. Whichever the case, we wear many hats,
and it isn't easy wearing them all at the same time. Whether we
are married or single, old or young, work inside or outside the
home, we have many responsibilities to juggle. We might even get
the knack of balancing the many roles of our homes, families and
church activities. But when a new responsibility is thrown upon
us, we lose our balance and concentration, things tumble around
us, and we have to start over.

Isn't there a better way to handle this juggling act and keep our
balance? We need to find ways to meet the challenge of balance
head-on. Maybe we need to slow our juggling rhythm. Maybe we
don't need to accept all the things thrown at us. Maybe we can juggle the ones we have with a better attitude.

We speak of balancing our checkbooks or accounting for our
money. We balance our diets (no, not a cookie in each hand!) by
eating a well-rounded diet. In a similar way, life balance means accounting for our lives and keeping them well-rounded. But why is
this equilibrium in our lives so difficult to achieve? Let's look at
some aspects of balance for some answers.

### Balance Is Complex

We live in a complicated society. Our world is full of frustrations
like computer viruses, long checkout lines, bumper-to-bumper
traffic, and junk mail. But we are blessed with well-stocked super
stores, home delivery, microwave ovens, and out-patient surgeries.
We are economically rich but emotionally and spiritually impov-
erished. We can talk by phone to someone on the other side of the
world, but we haven't talked to our next-door neighbor in months.
Achieving balance in our lives is difficult because so many factors
are involved. We can learn to simplify, not by throwing out technology, but by deciding what's important and focusing on that.

### Balance Is Individual

What balance is for you might not be balance for me. Your needs and wants are different from mine. What is peaceful for you might be pandemonium for me. For example, some women are very outgoing while others are reserved. Shy people need a break from people to regain their equilibrium. Other people would feel punished if they had to be by themselves for long. A woman should understand her unique temperament to keep her balance.

Imagine two opposite points with you somewhere in the middle. We fall somewhere between these extremes to reach our personal balance. Where do you usually fit between these points? Where would you be if you were living a more balanced life?

| | |
|---|---|
| SELF | OTHERS |
| WORK | PLAY |
| LEADING | FOLLOWING |
| SPEAKING | LISTENING |
| SOCIETY | SOLITUDE |
| LOGIC | INTUITION |
| STRUCTURE | SPONTANEITY |
| DISCIPLINE | FLEXIBILITY |
| PERSPIRATION | INSPIRATION |
| JUSTICE | MERCY [2] |

### Balance Is Ever-Changing

Life moves on. What was balance to us as teenagers or even five months ago is not balance now. Each stage and season in our lives brings new challenges that make us define balance a little differently. We grow and change with each passing year. Everyone around us is changing as well. It is a real feat just to keep up with the changing moods and stages in our families. Adapting to all these changes keeps us on the run.

## RATS ON THE RUN?

We don't have to be card-carrying members of "Rats on the Run." Instead of frantically heading nowhere fast, we can move ahead with purpose and direction. Our activity can be leveled out with a balance from above. We can switch lanes from the rat race to the more modulated Christian race, from the frenzied fast track to the faith track. We can lift our eyes to a higher goal than the accomplishment of the next task on our to-do lists.[3]

Someone has run this race before, and He will show us how. He experienced life on earth and knows what it is like. He dealt with sin in all its guises and can help to keep us from getting tripped up and entangled by the problems that we might encounter in our race. We need to concentrate on Him to keep our balance.

> Therefore, since we are surrounded by such a great cloud of witnesses, let us throw off everything that hinders and the sin that so easily entangles, and let us run with perseverance the race marked out for us. Let us fix our eyes on Jesus, the author and perfecter of our faith, who for the joy set before him endured the cross, scorning its shame, and sat down at the right hand of the throne of God. Consider him who endured such opposition from sinful men, so that you will not grow weary and lose heart (Hebrews 12:1-3).

We can find our focus in life. Sometimes we are running so fast that we lose sight of the purpose of our race. There are many things that can hold us back. We can become distracted by our overloaded lifestyles and sidetracked by the sins along the way. Jesus is our pacesetter, and He knows what we are facing. "To this you were called, because Christ suffered for you, leaving you an example, that you should follow in his steps" (1 Peter 2:21). Jesus' footprints are leading the way. He overcame and so can we. He can help us keep our balance. Toki Miyashina has penned a psalm to Jesus, our pacesetter in life's race.

### The Lord Is My Pacesetter

> The Lord is my pacesetter: I shall not rush. He makes me stop and rest for quiet intervals; He provides me with images of stillness, which restore my serenity. He leads me in ways of efficiency through great calmness of mind; and His guidance is peace. Even though I have a great

many things to accomplish each day, I will not fret, for His presence is here. His timelessness, His all-importance will keep me in balance. He prepares refreshment and renewal in the midst of my activity by anointing my mind with His oils of tranquility. My cup of joyous energy overflows. Surely, harmony and effectiveness shall be the fruits of all my hours, for I shall walk in the pace of my Lord, and dwell in His house forever.[4]

The Lord is our ultimate example of balance in every aspect of His life. "And Jesus grew in wisdom and stature, and in favor with God and men" (Luke 2:52). As a human, He felt frustration, anger and pressure, yet He found ways to balance the demands on His energy and time. We can look to Him to learn how to cope. Only by focusing on the life of Jesus and emulating His stride can we move beyond the rat race.

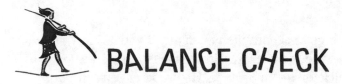

# BALANCE CHECK

*Summarize Hebrews 12:1-3 in your own words.*

1. Do you feel caught up in a rat race? In what specific ways?

2. What are some results from imbalance that you have seen in your life and the lives of others?

3. Why is it so difficult to maintain balance in life?

4. What are some of the roles you have to balance?

5. From these scriptures, how does a person keep his steps on the right track: Job 23:10-12; Psalm 37:23-24; 119:59-60; Proverbs 14:15; 20:24; Jeremiah 10:23?

6. How does Hebrews 11 give the background for 12:1-3?

7. What are some reasons the writer of Hebrews gives for focusing on Jesus as our example?

| | |
|---|---|
| Hebrews 1:1-4 | Hebrews 7:26-28 |
| Hebrews 3:1-6 | Hebrews 9:11-14 |
| Hebrews 4:14-16 | Hebrews 9:15 |
| Hebrews 5:7-10 | Hebrews 9:24-28 |
| Hebrews 7:23-25 | |

8. What are some examples in Scripture of ways Jesus was well-rounded spiritually, mentally, physically and socially?

9. How do Paul's references to running apply to the Christian race?

| | |
|---|---|
| Acts 20:24 | Galatians 5:7 |
| 1 Corinthians 9:24-27 | Philippians 2:14-18 |
| Galatians 2:2 | 2 Timothy 4:7 |

10. What encouragement is given in Isaiah 40:28-31 to God's people in life's race?

 # TIME OUT

*"There is more to life than increasing its speed."*
*– Mohandas Gandhi* [5]

*"It is an old and ironic habit of human beings to run faster when we have lost our way."*
*– Rollo May* [6]

*"Make haste slowly." – Benjamin Franklin* [7]

*"It isn't so much how busy you are, but why you are busy. The bee is praised; the mosquito is swatted."*
*– Unknown* [8]

*"Don't run through life so fast that you forget not only where you've been, but also where you are going." – Brian Dyson* [9]

*"The world is moving so fast these days that the man who says it can't be done is generally interrupted by someone doing it." – Elbert Hubbard* [10]

## CHAPTER 2

# OVERWHELMED

*"Let me not bite more off the cob than
I have teeth to chew." – Ogden Nash* [1]

Too much to do in too little time! Our society is plagued by an unprecedented overload – the phenomenon of "too much, too fast." There are many different kinds of overload, and they often impact each other. We are affected by some more directly than others:

• Change. For thousands of years, change tended to be slow and controlled. Now it moves at warp speed!

• Hurry. We live at a breathless, nonstop pace. We walk, talk and eat fast, and then as we leave say, "I must run."

• Activity. We busily fill our calendars weeks in advance and do several things at once to fit more into a day.

• Fatigue. We are a weary society. Even our back-to-back entertainment plans and scheduled vacations leave us tired instead of refreshed.

• Commitment. We take on too many jobs, friendships and committees to do them or ourselves justice. It is so difficult to just say no.

• Competition. The business world is more competitive than ever. At a younger age, children are competing more fiercely in academics and sports.

• Choice. Choices are everywhere! For example, 11,767 products were in the average grocery store in 1978. Now we have more than twice that many items to choose from, with more being developed.

• Decision. Whether the decisions are trivial or important, we now have more decisions to make and less time to make them.

• Education. The educational level rises each decade, but with more information to assimilate, we are falling increasingly behind.

• Information. More information is in a single edition of *The New York Times* than a 17th-century Englishman would see in a lifetime.

• Media. With 98 percent of American homes having television, the average family has two sets on seven hours a day. We can choose from more than 17,000 daily newspapers and 45,000 new book titles every year. Add to that the Internet.

• Technology. The average woman must operate an estimated 20,000 pieces of equipment in her lifetime. Some make our lives easier; others exasperate us!

• People. Each new day adds 250,000 people to our planet. Although we should love one another, overcrowding often leads to a loss of identity, rudeness and violence.

• Traffic. Rush hour has become neither a rush nor an hour. There are twice as many cars as people, with Americans driving two trillion miles every year.

• Noise. Fifty percent of Americans are exposed daily to noise interfering with their sleep or speech.

• Pollution. Billions of tons of carbon monoxide, smoke, smog, ozone, fertilizers, pesticides and other chemicals pollute our water, air and soil.

• Waste. America's 14,000 landfills are piling high and filling up too fast. Some of us throw away more food than some people exist on in a year.

• Possessions. We have more stuff than any society in history and still want more.

• Debt. From the government downward, we cannot seem to say no to spending.

- Work. We must work longer and harder to pay our debts, and more families are overworking and under-relating.
- Expectations. We are challenged to believe that we have no limits and no boundaries. Our expectations rise, and so does our guilt.
- Problems. With all this overload come problems – mental, physical, social and, most devastating, spiritual. Man seeks to solve all his problems on his own, but he can't. [2]

No wonder we are overwhelmed! As we look the 21st century in the face, life is probably not going to get any simpler. Unless we escape to a slower, less complicated culture, we must learn to balance our lives somehow.

## THE SUPERWOMAN MYTH

Some women try to cope with all this overload by taking on the role of Superwoman, the woman who can have it all, do it all, and be it all. Remember the comic book character Superman, who flew faster than a speeding bullet, leaped tall buildings with a single bound, and was more powerful than a locomotive? This Superwoman leaps piles of laundry at a single bound. She flies around the grocery store and grabs bargains faster than a speeding shopping cart.

Besides becoming more powerful in the office and the boardroom, she actively involves herself in school and community affairs and runs for public office. Her home is well-organized, creatively decorated and immaculate. Her made-from-scratch meals are always delicious, nutritious and on time. She sews all her children's clothes, teaches them French while she car pools them to music lessons and sports practices, and runs a cake-decorating business in her spare time. To top it off, after a long day, she still looks lovely and is ready to go on a sizzling date with her husband.

Wait a minute – does this Superwoman really exist? Or does her cape get a little droopy as some part of her well-orchestrated life begins to fall apart? Superwoman is just a myth, an ultimate women's fib, just as Superman is a comic book character. No woman can do it all, all the time.

What about the virtuous woman of Proverbs 31? Couldn't she qualify for Superwoman? After all, she was pretty close to doing it all – having a content husband and appreciative family, making their clothes, preparing handpicked food from the market, running a well-prepared household while she managed a little business on the side. Just reading about her causes us to suffer guilt and exhaustion! How could one woman do so much?

When we look closely at this energetic, got-it-all-together lady, we discover that she had servants to help her. She planned and coordinated her life, but she did not do all the work by herself. Also, this probably was not one day in the life of this woman, but rather a composite of what the role model of a well-rounded woman could be. That should be a comfort to us all. Just as Calvin Coolidge said, "We cannot do everything at once, but we can do something at once." ³

How about Paul's declaration in Philippians 4:13, "I can do everything through him who gives me strength"? Doesn't that mean we can do anything if Jesus is with us? Can we run nonstop for a day? Can we stay awake for a week without sleeping? Can we go a month without eating? No, there are certain limits that God placed upon us as humans. We are not blessed with infinite energy or inexhaustible strength. Even Jesus, as a human on earth, had to rest, eat and sleep. He did not work 24 hours a day, and He does not expect that of us.

Paul is rather affirming the Christian's real source of strength – Jesus. Whatever things I am able to do, I do through His power. Paul knew that God's power is made perfect in weakness (2 Corinthians 12:9). God gave us His power and strength to propel us to do His work, but He gave us limits to protect us.

## FEELING PERFECTLY GUILTY

Although some women might acknowledge their limits on the surface, deep down they think they have to do everything perfectly. These perfectionists are conscientious, dependable and goal-oriented, but are often extreme in their expectations. For instance, the perfectionist doesn't just clean out the bathroom closet. She spends days painting the inside, putting in new shelf paper, ironing and refolding all the linens, putting them back arranged by color and item, and alphabetizing the medicines. The closet looks beautiful when she is finished. Meanwhile, the laundry hamper overflows, the refrigerator is breeding green mold, and Junior has just painted the kitchen with ketchup!

The perfectionist spends too much time and works too hard on all her projects, many of which she does not finish. Some she does not even start – why try if she can't do it perfectly? She sets impossible goals and often projects her standards on others. When the perfectionist works so hard at being perfect and cannot achieve it, she feels like a failure. [4]

But doesn't Jesus urge us to "be perfect, therefore, as your heavenly Father is perfect" (Matthew 5:48)? Does that mean He demands perfection of us?

We can find the answer in the rich young ruler's encounter with Jesus. The Master told him, "If you want to be perfect, go, sell your possessions and give to the poor, and you will have treasures in heaven. Then come, follow me" (Matthew 19:21). Surely these actions would not make a perfect human, without flaw, out of this young man. Rather, he would be on the road to maturity and wholeness as a follower of Christ. The same is true for us. Jesus knows our frailties but exhorts us to aim high.

Besides bringing on a feeling of failure, unrealistic expectations can also lead to a false sense of guilt. There are two basic categories of guilt – real and imagined. Our guilt is real when we sin against God's law (Romans 3:23). Jesus provided a way to remove that guilt of sin. "If we claim to be without sin, we deceive ourselves and the truth is not in us. If we confess our sins, He is faithful and just and will forgive our sins and purify us from all unrighteousness" (1 John 1:8-9). God's forgiveness is complete; we need not carry the burden of guilt caused by our sins. Sometimes, however, we assume guilt where there is no wrongdoing. We lose our balance when we wallow in the mire of imagined shortcomings. [5]

Unrealistic standards of perfectionism and the resulting sense of failure and guilt can be overwhelming. No one can be perfect, but we can do our best. That is all that God asks of us.

## TRUE BALANCE

Where do we turn for a true sense of balance in our overloaded, out-of-kilter world? God is the epitome of order and balance. "For God is not a God of disorder but of peace" (1 Corinthians 14:33), and we see this clearly in His act of Creation. This was no glorious accident, but rather a very logical, organized and orderly process. Before the fall of man, the created world existed in perfect harmony and proportion.

God created humans to exist peacefully with a sense of balance with our surroundings and world. But when Adam and Eve sinned, this perfect balance was lost forever. After centuries of man's being overwhelmed by his sin and the problems of this world, God sent His Son to help us to find our balance again (Galatians 4:4-5). From Him, we can learn better how to balance our lives. Jesus comforts us with these words, "I have told you these things, so that in me you may have peace. In this world you will have trouble. But take heart! I have overcome the world" (John 16:33). With Him, we don't have to be overcome by this overwhelming world.

# BALANCE CHECK

*Summarize 2 Corinthians 6:3-10 in your own words.*

1. Which types of overload affect you most?
2. What can you do to lighten the effect of overload in your life?
3. What are some qualities of the virtuous woman in Proverbs 31? What can we learn from her example?
4. What did Paul mean by his declaration in Philippians 4:13?
5. What are some characteristics of a perfectionist?
6. Does Jesus expect perfection of us?
7. How can unrealistic expectations result in feelings of guilt and failure?
8. How did God demonstrate His sense of order and balance in Creation?
9. How did Adam and Eve ruin perfect balance in the world? What way did God provide for His people to find balance again?
10. When David was overwhelmed, to whom did he turn (Psalm 61:1-3)?

#  TIME OUT

*"Women aren't trying to do too much. Women have too much to do." – May Kay Blakely* [6]

*"Only a mediocre person is always at his best." – Somerset Maugham* [7]

*"Going beyond is as bad as falling short." – Chinese Folk Wisdom* [8]

*"Our life is frittered away by detail ... simplify, simplify." – Henry David Thoreau* [9]

*"There seems to be an excess of everything except parking space and religion." – Kin Hubbard* [10]

*"True happiness springs from moderation." – Johann Wolfgang von Goethe* [11]

**CHAPTER 3**

# CHOOSING THE BETTER PART

*"The hardest thing to learn in life is which bridge*
*to cross and which to burn." – David Russell* [1]

Decisions, decisions, decisions – some people have a difficult time making up their minds. Maybe they fear failure or change. They don't want to risk making the wrong choice, so they don't venture at all. They remind me of Samuel Goldwyn's quip, "True, I've been a long time making up my mind, but now I'm giving you a definite answer. I won't say yes and I won't say no – but I'm giving you a definite maybe." [2]

It is easy to see why we might hesitate to make decisions. In the American market we can choose from more than 1,200 varieties of shampoo, 2,000 skin-care products, and 64,000 videos. [3] The number of choices will continue to increase, making it even more difficult to make up our minds.

With so many choices, we do not always take the time we need to make wise decisions. We run from one activity to the next, reacting rather than choosing. When asked whether she wanted plastic or paper at the grocery store checkout, one lady answered, "You choose. I can't make another decision today."

When confronted with a decision, we don't always have to give instant answers. Statements such as "I'll get back to you" or "Let me pray about it" (if you intend to) will give us a chance to evalu-

ate what we should do. If possible, we should take the time to research information or investigate questions we might have before
we make a final choice. [4]

Some choices involve right and wrong, while others may not include moral or ethical issues. Still other decisions mean finding a
balance between two extremes. All decisions do not carry the same
weight. Choosing what to wear is certainly not as important as deciding to follow Jesus. Deciding upon a lifelong mate should require
more time and consideration than choosing a brand of mouthwash.
Some decisions have eternal implications, while others do not.

We should not painstakingly consider for hours what to wear or
what kind of mouthwash to use. But sometimes seemingly insignificant decisions can have a bearing on the most important ones.
If we wear dirty, frumpy clothes or have bad breath, we might have
less chance of finding someone suitable to marry. So although small
decisions do not carry the weight or require the time that larger
ones do, some decisions definitely matter. Let's look at two women
who made simple decisions that had spiritual implications.

## LOSING HER BALANCE

While Jesus and His disciples were traveling through Bethany,
they were invited to the home of Martha and her sister Mary.
Anyone who has had a crowd for dinner can understand Martha's
plight. She had at least 13 mouths to feed, and one was the Lord,
so not just anything would do. Everything had to be made from
scratch – no calling out for a pizza here! As Martha was busily
rushing, trying to prepare for her guests, she noticed that Mary
was just sitting at Jesus' feet and listening to His teaching. Martha,
frustrated by her sister's lack of help, brought this to the Lord's
attention. " 'Martha, Martha,' the Lord answered, 'You are wor-
ried and upset about many things, but only one thing is needed.
Mary has chosen what is better, and it will not be taken away from
her' " (Luke 10:41-42).

Martha was gracious in offering her hospitality to Jesus, but she
became more preoccupied with the meal than with the Master.
She was so busy working for Jesus that she didn't have time to be

with Him! Likely, in her excitement and hurry, she forgot to think about any other options she had. Perhaps she could have called others to help her. Or she might have listened to Jesus with Mary and then they both could have worked to prepare the meal together. Maybe she could have just prepared a simpler meal. [5]

Martha was so absorbed in her work that she lost her perspective and balance. She didn't want to seem like an uncaring hostess, so she went overboard in the other direction. Martha's decision impacted her relationship with God. So do our decisions. That's why learning to make wise decisions is so important.

## THE SOURCE OF WISDOM

If we lean on our own resources to make our decisions, the results can be disastrous. Fortunately, we can tap into the greatest decision-making resource around – the wisdom of God. God's wisdom is woven through His Word, and learning to put its precepts into practice is the key to successful decision-making.

Knowledge of God's Word is paramount in making decisions, but we need more than just knowledge of facts. Paul's prayer for the Philippians identifies another component for making decisions – depth of insight. He writes,

> And this is my prayer: that your love may abound more and more in knowledge and depth of insight, so that you may be able to discern what is best and may be pure and blameless until the day of Christ (Philippians 1:9-10).

But we can't just read the Bible and expect the wisdom to spill out like magical answers for each particular situation. One young man decided to seek God's will by opening up the Bible and reading what his finger first landed on. Convinced that God was leading him, he broke his first engagement and began dating another girl. The verse he read? "Then he said, 'Here I am, I have come to do your will.' He sets aside the first to establish the second" (Hebrews 10:9).

God will give us wisdom, but we have to ask for it with faith through prayer. Proverbs 2:3-6 states,

If you call out for insight and cry aloud for understanding, and if you look for it as for silver and search for it as for hidden treasure, then you will understand the fear of the LORD and find the knowledge of God. For the LORD gives wisdom, and from his mouth come knowledge and understanding.

James reiterates this idea:

If any of you lacks wisdom, he should ask God, who gives generously to all without finding fault, and it will be given to him. But when he asks, he must believe and not doubt, because he who doubts is like a wave of the sea, blown and tossed by the wind (James 1:5-6).

## PANIC, PONDER OR POPCORN?

When some people are faced with a decision, they panic. They have no basis on which to make choices and do not know where to start. Others know where to start, but they get no further because they ponder so long about the options they face.

Nicholas Comninellis, in his book *Where Do I Go to Get a Life?*, gives us some easy principles for decision-making with the mnemonic "POPCORN." [6]

**P**ray for Wisdom. Ask the Lord for help (Philippians 4:6-7).

List the **O**ptions. Write down your choices to make them clear (1 Chronicles 21:9-12).

Weigh the **P**ros. Consider the advantages ...

Weigh the **C**ons. ... and disadvantages (Luke 14:28-30).

**O**pen Your Bible. Study any appropriate scripture (Psalm 119:105).

Get **R**ecommendations. Seek advice from qualified people you trust (Proverbs 15:22).

**N**o hurry! Take your time to make a wise decision (Proverbs 21:5).

You would probably not use these guidelines for deciding if you should wash your car or get a haircut, but they would be appropriate as you consider many of life's decisions, especially the most important ones such as: Should I become a Christian? Should I marry? If so, whom? What talents do I have to offer? What is my unique purpose in life? What vocation should I follow?

We must not forget the most important step in making decisions – confidently acting on our decisions. Move ahead and don't look back. Sometimes we hesitate or worry if we have made a right choice. [7] James says a double-minded man is unstable in all he does (James 1:8).

We can learn to anchor our decisions by using our emotions and our logic. We cannot entirely rely on either our feelings or our intellect alone. We need to temper one with the other. By balancing both of these, however, we have a better chance of making wise choices.

The decisions could go on forever! Each decision is a personal one with a unique answer for each of us. But there is one decision that has the same answer for everyone. It is the most crucial question anyone can ask and the most important decision anyone can make. It is a free choice. No one forces you to make it. This one-time decision affects all others and sets the direction for the rest of your life. It is the decision to follow Christ. When we believe He is the Son of God, repent of the sins that separate us from Him, confess His name, and are buried in water as He was buried after His death, we become Christians. That decision is the most important of all.

May we make the same choice as Joshua when he proclaimed, "But if serving the LORD seems undesirable to you, then choose for yourselves this day whom you will serve. ... But as for me and my household, we will serve the LORD" (Joshua 24:15).

 BALANCE CHECK

*Summarize Proverbs 4:7-27 in your own words.*

1. Why is it often difficult to make decisions today? Why are some decisions more important than others? What is the most important decision a person can make?

2. In Luke 10, how did Mary and Martha's decisions affect them spiritually?

3. How can we tap into the wisdom of God? Why are both knowledge and understanding important?

4. Using the mnemonic POPCORN, what are some principles for wise decision-making?

5. What did Gad encourage David to do before the king had to decide on the punishment of Israel after he counted the fighting men (2 Samuel 24:13)?

6. Why did Jesus say His decisions of judgment are right (John 8:16)?

7. What choice was Paul torn between (Philippians 1:21-26)?

8. What were the far-reaching results of the decisions made by the Bible characters in these Scriptures?

Genesis 3:6-7      Genesis 34:1-7
Genesis 6:18-22    Genesis 37:17-20
Genesis 11:3-4     Exodus 2:1-10
Genesis 12:4-5     Esther 4:15-16
Genesis 16:1-4     John 10:14-18
Genesis 25:29-34

9. How is the wisdom of Solomon described (1 Kings 4:29-34)?

10. Charles Hummel said, "Lone Ranger decision-making and action reflect the individualism of our culture." Should that kind of decision-making describe Christians?

 # TIME OUT

*"Don't swap horses when you are crossing a stream."* – Abraham Lincoln [8]

*"Through indecision opportunity is often lost."* – Latin proverb [9]

*"When possible make the decisions now, even if action is in the future. A reviewed decision usually is better than one reached at the last moment."* – William B. Given [10]

*"He who considers too much will perform little."* – German proverb [11]

*"The best time to make a decision is before you have to make one."* – Unknown [12]

*"When you have to make a choice and don't make it, that in itself is a choice."* – William James [13]

## CHAPTER 4

# ROCKS IN YOUR JAR

*"All men should strive to learn before they die
what they are running from, and to, and why."*
*– James Thurber* [1]

O ne day a time management expert was illustrating a point to a group of business students. He filled a gallon jar with fist-sized rocks and asked them, "Is the jar full?"

"Yes," the class said in agreement.

Then he said, "Are you sure?" He then poured in a bucket of gravel and shook the jar to get the gravel pieces crammed in any leftover spaces. "Is the jar full now?" he questioned.

"Probably not," someone had figured out.

"You're right!" Then he brought out a bucket of sand and filled up every empty crevice. "Is the jar full?"

The class shouted, "No!"

"Good," he smiled and then began to pour a pitcher of water in the jar until it was filled to the brim.

"What's the point of this illustration?" he asked.

One eager beaver ventured, "The point is that, even if your schedule if full already, you can always fit in something else."

"No," the expert replied. "The point is that if you don't place the big rocks in the jar first, you can't put them in later." [2]

It is crucial that we first make a place for the big rocks in our lives, those things that are the most important to us. Only by setting priorities for the big rocks first can we find a place for them.

Whether we think about them or write them down, we all have priorities. We will know what they are by how we spend our time, money and effort. Do you love a sport or hobby? Are you a workaholic? Are the Lord and His church important to you? How about your family? The way we live tells us what our priorities are. What are your priorities?

## ALL, FIRST, BEST

From the beginning of Creation, God has desired His people's utmost obedience and first allegiance. Secondhand and second-best would not do. The superlatives "all," "first" and "best" were used to describe the devotion God desires from His people. The Jews were commanded to bring God their best animals (Leviticus 22:17-25; Numbers 18:29) and their finest of first fruits for sacrifice (Exodus 23:19). Jesus in the Sermon on the Mount told His listeners, "But seek first His kingdom and His righteousness, and all these things will be given to you as well" (Matthew 6:33). We put Him first because He loved us first and sent Jesus to save us (John 3:16). We give Him all because He has blessed us with every spiritual blessing in Christ (Ephesians 1:3).

But ultimately, how do you serve God in practical terms? If you had one command or priority, what would it be?

An expert in the law had the same question. The rabbis of Jesus' time would argue back and forth, trying to decide which of Moses' commandments was the most important. They had counted 613 different laws, and of those, 365 were negative and 248 positive with some "heavy" and others "light"! [3] This expert ventured to ask Jesus to settle the issue once and for all. He was asking Jesus for a condensed version of what it took to please God.

> Jesus replied, "Love the Lord your God with all your heart and with all your soul and with all your mind." This is the first and greatest commandment. And the second is like it: "Love your neighbor as yourself." All the Law and the Prophets hang on these two commandments (Matthew 22:37-39).

Note that the questioner asked for the greatest commandment, but Jesus gave him two. In reality, these commands are inseparable. One without the other is impossible. We cannot love God without loving our neighbor. We cannot love our neighbor without loving God. And we are to love ourselves the same as our neighbor. So, in a nutshell, the expert was told to love, that is the greatest way to please God.

So Jesus emphasized that loving God, others and ourselves is a priority. How does this translate into daily life? We have obligations to our families, our jobs, the church and the community. And we must not forget ourselves! How do we as Christians keep all the demands of our lives in balance? Where does everything fit?

# FITTING IT ALL IN

Many Christians have tried to use a hierarchy for priorities: God first, family second, church third, work fourth, the community fifth, and self last. While these initially sound good, they tend to give the impression that we will always face an either/or situation. Without a doubt, God should always come first and family is important. But will we ever face a dilemma to follow God *or* feed our family? Or should we always sacrifice for everyone else, continually leaving ourselves last? Each of these areas of life is important, and we do not want to stop or neglect one to do another.

Fortunately, we do not have to stop loving God to love our families. Being good to others should not mean neglecting ourselves. We must learn to balance these roles in our lives. We can serve God *as* we serve the church, family, community, work and our own needs. Keeping our balance is learning what to do when. Setting priorities can help us do just that. [4]

In setting priorities, it is important to realize that God is not just one of our priorities. He is *the* priority. He is the Lord of our lives, permeating our actions whether we are negotiating a deal, drying an eye, or kneeling in prayer. It helps us to see God in the center of our lives with His love radiating to everyone and everything that touches us. We can show this with God in the center of the figure of a star (see figure 1), with the other five areas touching that center. Each of these five areas covers a different facet of our lives. [5]

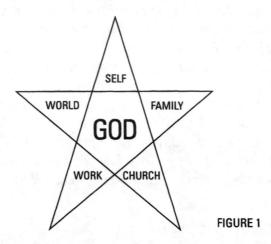

FIGURE 1

Even when we set priorities, we will probably be confronted with conflicting options. The answers won't always be clear-cut, but we will have a basis upon which to choose. We might ask ourselves these questions: How can I best serve the Lord right now? At this stage of my life, will this activity work in these circumstances? How are my relationships now? Does one area need attention? How will the activity in question affect my relationships later? Am I overcommitted? How much energy and time do I have? How much will this activity take? What will happen if I don't participate in this activity? Will it matter later? In the long run, will it count for eternity? [6]

## SAYING NO TO SAY YES

Sometimes one of the hardest things to say is "no." When people ask us to do something, we hate to let them down. Yet in keeping with our priorities, sometimes we must say no. Benjamin Franklin stated, "One-half the trouble of this life can be traced to saying yes too quick, and not saying no soon enough." [7]

We cannot please everyone or do everything. Even Jesus, when He was on earth, found that He had to say no in order to have the time and energy to fulfill His mission. He was on earth to please

His Father rather than Himself (John 6:38; 8:28-29). He had only three short years for service, and He had to ever keep His priorities in mind.

Let's look at one hectic day in the life of Jesus. He began it by teaching in the synagogue in Capernaum and healing a man possessed by an evil spirit. Then, upon leaving the synagogue, He went to Simon and Andrew's home, where Jesus healed Simon's mother-in-law. After sunset, He continued to heal the sick and demon-possessed. People were lined up at the door into the night. Mark 1:35-39 reads:

> Very early in the morning, while it was still dark, Jesus got up, left the house and went off to a solitary place, where he prayed. Simon and his companions went to look for him, and when they found him, they exclaimed: "Everyone is looking for you!" Jesus replied, "Let us go somewhere else – to the nearby villages – so I can preach there also. That is why I have come." So he traveled through Galilee, preaching in their synagogues and driving out demons.

Although Jesus was needed by "everyone" in Capernaum, Jesus knew there were other people who needed His message and healing as well. His purpose was to reach everyone He possibly could, but He could not do that if He stayed. He had to say no to Capernaum in order to say yes to the nearby villages. [8]

It probably wasn't easy for Jesus to say no. It isn't easy for us either. But it will be worse if we continue to take on more than we can realistically handle or desire to do. Always saying yes can result in burnout, stress, depression, anxiety, resentment and anger. Saying no does not mean laziness or resistance to try something new, but rather a genuine need or desire to do something else. Saying no means saying yes to the important things.

What are some ways you can decline politely but firmly when requests are made and you have other priorities? Honestly say you cannot handle any more activities at this time because of prior commitments. Suggest other qualified people who can do the job when you cannot. Check your family's schedules so you will know their activities before you have to make a commitment. It is frustrating to everyone concerned when you commit yourself and then have to bow out later. Do not say maybe when you really mean no. Tell the truth up front. The person asking you will appreciate your honesty in the long run. Do not feel guilty when you say no. Even if you have planned something simple like spending time with your family, you have even more reason not to feel obligated to say yes. Accept no from others as well. No one, not even Jesus, has to say yes all the time! [9]

Dwight Eisenhower said, "The urgent is seldom important, and the important seldom urgent." [10] We rush around majoring in minors and letting life slip through our fingers. We do not have to be so torn apart by life's demands. We can find direction in the comprehensive balance found in God's Word. Doug Sherman and William Hendricks agree: "Christians do not need to be fragmented, mechanistic, schizophrenic people rushing neurotically from one activity to another. Instead, we can pursue a well-rounded, healthy life that sets limits, yet enjoys the freedom that comes from balance." [11] Priorities can keep us balanced, but only when we have a plan.

# BALANCE CHECK

*Summarize Matthew 6:25-34 in your own words.*

1. How do we show what our priorities are?
2. In what ways did God demand the superlatives "all," "first" and "best" from His people?
3. How did Jesus answer the expert in the law regarding the greatest commandment?
4. Why did Jesus give the expert two commands instead of one?
5. Why does it help to look at God as the center of our lives?
6. What are some useful questions to ask when we set priorities?
7. In Mark 1, why did Jesus refuse to stay longer in Capernaum?
8. What are some other occasions when Jesus said no to say yes (Luke 2:49; 5:15-16; John 5:1-13; 7:6-9)?
9. Discuss some tactful ways we can say no.
10. What did Seneca mean when he said, "If a man does not know to what port he is steering, no wind is favorable to him"?

 # TIME OUT

*"We need to know what our priorities are to act on them, but they're not really priorities* unless *we act on them." – Kathy Peel* [12]

*"If you aim at nothing, chances are you'll hit it." – Unknown* [13]

*"Saddle your dreams before you ride them." – Mary Webb* [14]

*"Objectives that matter the most must never be at the mercy of things that matter least." – Johann Wolfgang von Goethe* [15]

*"Horse-sense is 'stable' thinking hitched up with the ability to say 'Nay.' " – Unknown* [16]

*"Resist doing things which have no meaning for life." – Pablo Casals* [17]

## CHAPTER 5

# HOW CRAZY IS YOUR QUILT?

*"Hundreds of scattered, unrelated stimulating frag-*
*ments, each going off in its own direction, creating a lot*
*of frantic energy. There was no overall structure to hold*
*the pieces together. The Crazy Quilt was a perfect*
*metaphor for my life." – Sue Bender* [1]

For centuries, quilts have provided decoration and warmth with a myriad of fabric, designs and colors. Our ancestors would laugh if they could see some of the exorbitant prices these pieces of Americana bring at auction today.

Although they are now considered handcrafted imprints of historical importance, back then women were just using scraps of fabric to piece together some warmth for their families. Some of these women would plan to piece their fabric into definite patterns, such as the Wedding Ring or the Star of Texas. Other ladies would piece whatever scraps they had into random patterns, never knowing exactly what would be the outcome. These were called crazy quilts.

Some people live their lives like crazy quilts. They are just thrown together as they go along. They have no idea how their lives will turn out because they have no plan.

## AN OUNCE OF PLANNING ...

"We don't believe in planning," says Dr. Raymond Havelick, director of the Institute for Psychosomatic Research in Roslyn, N.Y. "We are a crisis-oriented civilization. We react after the crisis and typically the reaction to make things better is patchwork and rarely deals with the underlying forces." [2]

"Plan" to some people is a four-letter word. They think, why waste the time to plan when life is for the living now? So they live life on the edge, only for the present.

Some people even say the Bible does not support planning. They cite James 4:13-17, which says,

> Now listen, you who say, "Today or tomorrow we will
> go to this or that city, spend a year there, carry on busi-
> ness and make money." Why, you do not even know
> what will happen tomorrow. What is your life? You are
> a mist that appears for a little while and then vanishes.
> Instead, you ought to say, "If it is the Lord's will, we will
> live and do this or that." As it is, you boast and brag. All
> such boasting is evil. Anyone, then, who knows the good
> he ought to do and doesn't do it, sins.

In this scripture, rather than condemning planning ahead, James is condemning boasting about plans when life is so uncertain. We should be sure we are acting within God's will and put our plans in His hands. "Do not those who plot evil go astray? But those who plan what is good find love and faithfulness" (Proverbs 14:22).

Jesus commended the person who plans ahead. He told of the tower builder and the warring king who both had to count the cost of what they were doing before they could commit themselves (Luke 14:28-33). In the same way, a woman has to look ahead and ask herself, "Am I willing to give up everything to follow Christ?" This decision cannot be a knee-jerk reaction but one with thought and planning.

Notice in the above scripture that each of the men Jesus mentioned had to sit down and estimate or consider. That's the reason many of us do not plan – we do not want to take the time to sit down and think! It has been shown, however, that an ounce of planning is worth a pound of intervention after the fact. We can actually save time and trouble in the long run if we plan ahead.

## GOALING FOR IT

Proverbs 16:3 states, "Commit to the LORD whatever you do, and your plans will succeed." To help make our plans succeed, we need to set some goals, preferably written down. Goals have been called dreams with deadlines. Setting goals is our chance to dream. Making some lifetime goals is a good place to start. Ask yourself: At the end of my life, what do I want to have accomplished? In each of my different roles, what do I want to do?

It has been said that goals written down have a 90 percent greater chance of succeeding. Writing down goals helps us to remember them and impress them into our minds. Experts tell us to write down everything so we do not have to tax our memory.

It's like the elderly man who was dating the widow and finally asked her to marry him. But the next day he couldn't remember how she had answered. After about an hour, he gave up and telephoned her. Embarrassed, he admitted that he couldn't remember her answer to his proposal.

"Oh, I'm so glad to hear from you," she replied. "I remember saying yes to someone, but I couldn't for the life of me remember who it was!" [3]

It is important to set short-term goals too. These will help us attain those long-range goals step by step. These goals can cover everything from cleaning your house to devoting more time to your family to becoming a better employee at work. Do you want to have a better relationship with your parents? Go on a mission trip? Learn a new language? Become a better cook? Teach a Bible class? Make it a goal.

It might help to make these in the five areas of our priorities. Let's look at some sample long-range and short-term goals we might make concerning ourselves, our families, our church, our work and our efforts to interact with the world.

*Self*
1. Grow in the knowledge of the Scriptures. (long-range)
2. Read the Bible 15 minutes daily. (short-term)

*Family*
1. Plan more activities for family togetherness.
2. Put photographs in albums next weekend.

*Church*
1. Get better acquainted with and encourage new members
   of our congregation.
2. Have lunch with new Christian _____ next week.

*Work*
1. Be more punctual.
2. Leave home no later than 7:40 every morning to get to
   work on time.

*World*
1. Be more evangelistic.
2. Learn more about sharing the gospel from a training class
   this year. [4]

Be sure that you can take responsibility for your goals. You cannot assume total responsibility for having a better marriage, but
you can try to be a better wife by listening more attentively to your
husband. Your children might not always be able to win their soc-
cer games, but you can be there to support them. You might not
be able to have a better relationship with your mother, but you can
call or write her every week to show you care. You have responsibility only for the goals you can control. [5]

Brainstorm what is on your mind, and try to think of solutions
through your goals. Questions like these might help:

• If I had only a month to live, how would I live?

• What bothers me the most right now? Can I change it? If I
can't change it, can I find a better way to deal with it?

But how can we know if we have reached our goals? We can measure our progress if we remember that our goals should be SMART.

**S**pecific – Set definite objectives, not just general ones.

**M**easurable – Measure progress in terms of amount or degree.

**A**chievable – Set possible goals within our age and ability.

**R**esourceful – Utilize the resources and talents we have.

**T**imed – Set deadlines to avoid procrastination. [6]

Now that our goals are on paper, the real challenge is accomplishing them. It helps to have someone with whom we can share our goals. That person can encourage us when we fail and rejoice with us when we succeed. We should also periodically update our goals when circumstances change or when objectives are attained.

Keep flexible. Sometimes interruptions and accidents keep us from achieving all we would like to accomplish. That isn't always bad. Serendipity, the surprises in our lives that we don't plan, can bring us a lot of joy. Just ask any 45-year-old mother with a new baby! If we have an idea where we are headed in our lives, a few detours should not send us in the wrong direction. Oliver Wendell Holmes Sr., said, "The great thing in this world is not so much where we are, but in what direction we are moving." [7]

## PLANNING TOOLS

Now that you have set some goals, how can you easily keep up with them and how you are doing? Many women find it helpful to chart their progress in notebooks, flippers, cards, files and clipboards. Let's look at some of the ways these can be used.

• Notebooks. Notebooks come in all shapes and sizes. How much better to have a notebook than 50 pieces of paper by the phone, in your purse, and in the car. You can include any kind of section that you desire. Here are some possibilities: Calendar, Goals, Prayer List, Sermon Notes, Family, Home Decorating, Personal, Career, Physical, Service and Financial. Notebooks are the perfect place for noting the sizes and gift ideas of your family and ideas you might have for your home. If it fits in your purse, you can have all this information with you when you need it.

• Flippers. Flippers are photo albums with sleeves the size of 3-by-5 inch cards. On these you can list the housecleaning goals of the day, mark them off with an erasable marker, and then flip over for the next day's goals.

• Cards. Index cards can be used in a file box. Daily, weekly, monthly and yearly jobs are listed by colors, by day of the week or by the month. When jobs are completed, they are filed and used again when needed.

• Files. Filing systems numbered 1-31 for every day of the month as well as alphabetical files could be used as a "tickler file" for sending back school papers, mailing bills and cards, and filing recipes.

• Clipboards. Weekly menus, shopping lists, clothing needs, coupons, and ongoing to-do lists can be conveniently clipped together. Children can even be given their own smaller clipboards.[8]

You can utilize one or more of these methods. Before you spend a lot of money and time on any one method, experiment with each. Any system, no matter how simple or sophisticated, is not worth the trouble if it doesn't work for you.

## THE ULTIMATE PLANNER

In stores you might see all kinds of organizational planners with all kinds of accessories to plan your life. Some might even be called the ultimate in planners. But there is only one Ultimate Planner, and that is God. God had a well-designed plan for making the world. He had a plan for saving the world through Jesus Christ. Through the prophet Jeremiah, He told the nation of Israel,

> "For I know the plans I have for you," declares the LORD, "plans to prosper you and not to harm you, plans to give you hope and a future. Then you will call upon me and come and pray to me, and I will listen to you. You will seek me and find me when you seek me with all your heart" (Jeremiah 29:11-13).

If God had plans for the bedraggled nation of Israel in Babylonian captivity, then He certainly has plans for us!

# BALANCE CHECK

*Summarize Luke 14:28-33 in your own words.*

1. Why is it sometimes difficult to make plans in our society?
2. How does the Bible support planning ahead in these scriptures: Proverbs 14:22; 16:3; Luke 14:28-33?
3. What do Proverbs 27:1 and James 4:13-17 teach about planning ahead?
4. Why are goals like dreams with deadlines?
5. Why is it helpful to write our goals down?
6. How should our goals be SMART?
7. Why is it important to be flexible with our goals?
8. Discuss some planning tools that have helped you focus on your goals.
9. What are some things that God planned for in the Bible?
10. What will help our plans have a better chance of succeeding (Proverbs 15:22; 20:18)?

 # TIME OUT

*Life is what happens to us while we are making other plans." – Thomas La Mance* [9]

*"Make no little plans; they have no magic to stir men's blood. Make big plans, aim high in hope and work." – Daniel H. Burnham* [10]

*"Make your year's plans in the spring, and your day's plans early in the morning."
– Henry Hersch Hart* [11]

*"You must have long-range goals to keep you from being frustrated by short-term failures."
– Charles C. Noble* [12]

*"Arriving at one goal is the starting point to another." – John Dewey* [13]

*"No specific goal can sustain one for very long after it is achieved." – Adam Smith* [14]

**CHAPTER 6**

# TIME MATTERS

*"Too often I feel like an Egyptian mummy*
*– pressed for time."– Glen Martin* [1]

**I**f only there were more hours in a day." How many times have we thought that? What would happen if we were to wake up one morning and have 30 hours in our day? Would we live any differently? Would we squeeze in even more activities? Would we take the extra time and do some things we have wanted to do but never had the time? Or would we spend more time improving our spiritual lives by reading the Bible and praying?

The fact is that we only have 24 hours in our day – 86,400 golden seconds. Time is the only commodity in which everyone is blessed equally. People might have varying amounts of money or talent, but their time is all the same. We speak of losing, finding, making and saving time, but actually all we can do is manage better the time we have.

Think about how you spend your precious 24 hours everyday. Sleep time alone accounts for six to eight hours each day. How many years would that amount to in your lifetime? Mark Porter, in his book *The Time of Your Life* provides an estimate on how people would spend their time if they lived to be 75 years old (see figure 2).

FIGURE 2 [2]

| Years | Activity | % of Time |
|-------|----------|-----------|
| 23 | Sleeping | 31 |
| 19 | Working | 25 |
| 9 | Amusements (TV, etc.) | 12 |
| 7½ | Dressing and Personal Care | 10 |
| 6 | Eating | 8 |
| 6 | Traveling | 8 |
| ½ | Worshiping and Praying | 0.7 |

Were you surprised at the breakdown of time? Though different people may vary, it probably holds true that we spend more time in certain activities than we think. How about our time spent worshiping and praying? When I estimated a weekly average of five hours of worship and prayer (4 hours of worship and 1 hour of prayer), the percentage was 0.03!

No wonder Paul told the Ephesians,

> Be very careful, then, how you live – not as unwise but as wise, making the most of every opportunity, because the days are evil. Therefore do not be foolish, but understand what the Lord's will is (Ephesians 5:15-17).

With the rampant nature of evil, we should take advantage of every opportunity to do good and learn what God's will is. We have no time to waste!

Does that mean every minute should be used to pray, read the Bible, teach the lost, and attend church services? Jesus did all these things, yet He balanced the activities of His life. We see Him sleeping in a storm, joining a wedding celebration, and serving His disciples breakfast. Although Jesus focused on His mission, He used His time wisely to include solitude, relaxation and fellowship. Jesus knew only too well His purpose, but He was never in too much of a hurry to listen and help. He knew that His time was short and had to be used productively. He told His disciples, "As long as it is day, we must do the work of him who sent me. Night is coming, when no one can work" (John 9:4).

# SLICING YOUR PIE

Let's deal with some general principles that can help us balance our time. Our time could be compared to a pie with everyone getting the same size. How will we slice it? How much time will we spend for God, others or ourselves? It all depends on how much of the pie we "*ate*."

• Alloc*ate* daily planning time. You may make grandiose goals, but take a few minutes to plan how you will carry through on them. The time you spend in thoughtful planning will pay off in effectiveness.

• Abbrevi*ate* your goals. Write your long-term and short-term goals in shortened form where you will see them often so they will keep you focused. [3]

• Estim*ate* the time a job will take, and then add some. If you need more time, you will have it. If you finish early, you can reward yourself with the leftover time. [4]

• Concentr*ate*. Jesus did not waste His energy but concentrated on His reason for coming to earth. Likewise, we need to concentrate on our priorities to maximize our effectiveness.

• Regener*ate* your body by taking advantage of your body's natural rhythms. Are you an early bird or a night owl? Are you a zombie by 11 p.m., or does it take until noon for you to wake up? To be more productive, plan your most brain-intensive work when you are alert.

• Appreci*ate* the little chunks of time. Think of all the things you can do in 10 minutes – sew on a button, send a card, pray.

• Evalu*ate* your expectations. Are you too critical of yourself and others? Do you have to do tasks over because the results are not perfect? Relax a little if your standards are too high. Remember, there will never be enough time to get everything done!

• Deleg*ate*. If we need help, we should ask for it from our families, co-workers and friends. Jesus delegated when He chose 12, and later 70, men to help Him spread the Good News. When we share tasks with others, our burdens will be lightened.

This delegation and sharing reminds me of the elderly couple who shared everything in their lives. They shared their chores

50/50. They shared their belongings 50/50. They even shared
their meals 50/50. They were in a restaurant and ordered one
meal, halving everything. Someone saw the man was eating while
his wife waited patiently. When asked why she had to wait, she
replied that it was her husband's turn with the teeth!

• Alternate disagreeable jobs with pleasant ones to get more accomplished. Mop the floor (which you dislike) before you start to
sew (which you enjoy). Don't save all your big chores for Saturday;
spread them out over the week if you can.

• Eliminate needless interruptions. Sometimes this is difficult, if not impossible. Value people and their needs, but value yourself as well by tactfully placing limits on your time. Determine ways
to let people know when you are available or not. Of course, this
does not apply to emergencies. Jesus' life was full of interruptions
– a little man popping out of a sycamore tree, children swarming
all over Him, a blind man's earnest shouts for mercy. The Lord
didn't dismiss any of these, but still found time away when He
needed to renew Himself.

• Uncomplicate. Cut unessential activities. The more clutter
in our lives, the more time it takes to deal with them. Simplify
everything you can. Sometimes technology is more complicated
than we need – for example, the food chopper that is more trouble to clean that it is worth.

• Consolidate your errands to maximize your travel time. Why
backtrack when you can pick up the dry-cleaning, stop by the post
office, and drop off the library books in one trip.

• Automate. Let technology work for you so you work smarter,
not harder. Call ahead to make a reservation. Use the Internet to
place a hold on a library book. Use appliances to save time and work.

• Isolate yourself when you occasionally need to be alone. Some
weary moms go to a park or restaurant to have a quiet time with
God. Let your family know by some sign (like a closed door) if you
need some privacy to regain your balance. Sometimes Jesus isolated Himself from the crowds that pressed at Him.

• Reevaluate every so often the way you use your time. Circumstances change. What works best now for this stage of your life? [5]

## SLOSHING THROUGH THE SWATCHES

"Funny how we get so exact about time at the end of life and at its beginning. She died at 6:08 p.m., we say, or the baby was born at 4:02 a.m. But in between we slosh through huge swatches of time – weeks, months, years, decades even," says Helen Prejean. [6] Especially as we get older, events just seem to merge together unless we make some of them special.

The Yakima tribe in the Northwestern United States had an interesting custom. When a girl of their tribe reached puberty, she began her "time ball" or "counting the days ball," which was much like a diary. For every significant life event, she tied a knot, with sometimes a bead or shell, in a piece of hemp string. She finally wound it into a ball. This time ball became a tangible record of her life, beginning with her first courtship, marriage, birth of her children, and other events up until her death, at which time the ball was buried with her. In this way, she remembered the special moments of her life. [7]

What are we doing to capture the significant events of our lives? Often we women lose our identity in our families or our work. We live on the achievements of our husbands, our children or the organizations we work for without fully appreciating our own accomplishments or memories. How can we celebrate our personal lives with our own kind of time balls?

Some women keep journals that record the highs and lows of their lives. These can be valuable for expressing inner thoughts, but also for realizing how special even the ordinary days are. Photo albums, audio recordings, and videos serve as permanent ways to remember as well. The popularity of scrapbooking proves that more and more women want to remember the significant, and seemingly insignificant, days of their lives.

## NOW IS THE TIME

The author of Ecclesiastes wrote, "He has made everything beautiful in its time. He has also set eternity in the hearts of men; yet they cannot fathom what God has done from beginning to end" (Ecclesiastes 3:11). God has given us each precious day to celebrate and enjoy. "This is the day the LORD has made; let us rejoice and be glad in it" (Psalm 118:24). We need to begin now to appreciate every day, whether it is a red-letter day or not. We need to utilize each day for God's glory and to live with a sense of eternity in our hearts. Only the things we do for God will really matter, and we need to start now!

Many people do not want to face doing anything "now." "Later" is more comfortable for them. A prime example of this procrastination in the Bible is the ruler Felix, who grew afraid when he heard Paul's discourse on righteousness, self-control and the judgment to come. Felix told Paul, "That's enough for now! You may leave. When I find it convenient, I will send for you" (Acts 24:25). Although Felix sent for Paul frequently, the Bible never records that he obeyed Paul's gospel message. The "convenient" time, as far as we know, never came, and he was lost forever.

We hope procrastination will not have such a devastating effect for us, but it can still result in turmoil and stress in our daily lives. How do we ward off this great time bandit? We can set firm dates and times to start projects. It might help to identify potential obstacles to beginning or doing the job and try to find solutions. Sometimes writing down the steps and breaking a big job into smaller pieces helps make the task seem less distasteful. Be accountable to someone to whom you can report your progress. Reward yourself at intervals and especially when you are finished. Try to get in the habit of doing something today, instead of tomorrow. [8]

We need to cherish the time we have now while we remember the past and look forward to the future. We don't need to bury our souls in the past, obsessing on the nostalgic good old days. Neither should we always lose our head in the clouds, dreaming of how great things will be when we … graduate, get married, have children, become successful in our jobs, become grandparents, retire.

Paul urges, "I tell you, now is the time of God's favor, now is the day of salvation" (2 Corinthians 6:2). The writer of Hebrews echoes the urgency of this sentiment: "But encourage one another daily, as long as it is called Today, so that none of you may be hardened by sin's deceitfulness" (Hebrews 3:13). The present is all we really have to do God's work. After explaining the uselessness of worry and the ultimate care of God for His children, Jesus encouraged us to focus on today: "Therefore do not worry about tomorrow, for tomorrow will worry about itself. Each day has enough trouble of its own" (Matthew 6:34). We can balance our outlook of time by concentrating on today.

## THE BANK OF TIME

An unknown author wrote:

> Imagine there is a bank that credits your account with $86,400. It carries over no balance from day to day. Every evening deletes whatever part of the balance you failed to use during the day. What would you do? Draw out every cent, of course! Each of us has such a bank. Its name is TIME. Every morning, it credits you with 86,400 seconds. Every night it writes off, as lost, whatever of this you have failed to invest to good purpose. It carries over no balance. It allows no overdraft. Each day it opens a new account for you. Each night it burns the remains of the day. If you fail to use the day's deposits, the loss is yours. There is no going back. There is no drawing against the "tomorrow." You must live in the present on today's deposits. Invest it so as to get from it the utmost in health, happiness, and success. The clock is running. Make the most of today. And remember that time waits for no one. Yesterday is history. Tomorrow is mystery. Today is a gift. That's why it's called the present! [9]

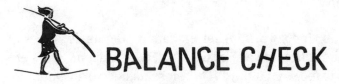

# BALANCE CHECK

*Summarize Ecclesiastes 3:1-8, 11 in your own words.*

1. Why should we make the most of every opportunity (Deuteronomy 33:25; Ephesians 5:15-17)?

2. Using the "*ate*'s" in the chapter, what specific ways can you implement better time management in your life?

3. Who delegated in these scriptures: Genesis 37:12-14; Exodus 18:13-26; Matthew 10:1-16; Acts 6:1-6?

4. How did Jesus deal with interruptions?

5. Why is it important to periodically evaluate your expectations?

6. What are some ways to utilize little chunks of time?

7. Share some ways you record the highs and lows of your life?

8. What was Paul's attitude in Philippians 3:12-14 about the past, present and future?

9. How does Paul explain the urgency of the Christian's action in the present in Romans 13:11-14?

10. What unusual miracles regarding changes in time occurred in the Bible (Joshua 10:13; 2 Kings 20:1-11; Mark 15:33-34)?

 # TIME OUT

*"All the treasures of earth cannot bring back one lost moment." – French proverb* [10]

*"Enjoy the little things, for one day you may look back and realize they were the big things."*
*– Robert Brault* [11]

*"Time is a circus always packing up and moving away." – Ben Hecht* [12]

*"Dost thou love life? Then do not squander time, for time is the stuff life is made of." – Benjamin Franklin* [13]

*"I recommend you to take care of the minutes, for the hours will take care of themselves." – Lord Chesterfield* [14]

*"Nothing is ours except time." – Seneca* [15]

## CHAPTER 7

# SAVE, SCRIMP OR SQUANDER?

*"Money may be the husk of many things, but not the
kernel. It brings you food, but not appetite; medicine,
but not health; acquaintances, but not friends; servants,
but not faithfulness; days of joy, but not peace
or happiness." – Henrik Ibsen* [1]

Three-year-old Polly was testing things by putting them in her
mouth. Before her mother could stop her, she plopped a nickel in and swallowed it. When her mother rushed over and pounded her back, Polly coughed up two dimes. Her mother frantically shouted to her husband, "What should we do? Polly's swallowed a nickel and coughed up two dimes!"

Her father yelled back, "We could use the money – keep feeding her nickels!" [2]

From the first time a baby tries to cram his toes in his mouth, it seems there is always a struggle to make both ends meet! [3] Money is not easy to make, but it is extremely easy to spend. Yearly, Americans spend three to four times more time shopping than Western Europeans. [4]

The average American at every income level – poor, middle-class and rich – buys more than twice as much as he or she did almost 50 years ago. [5] We are spending a higher fraction of our income. Buying on credit induces us to spend more than we have. [6] The shopping cart has become the most expensive vehicle, per mile, to operate! [7] Will Rogers quipped, "Too many people spend money they haven't earned, to buy things they don't want, to impress people they don't like." [8]

Our coins say "In God We Trust," but many people in our society are trusting in their coins instead. God's Word tells us how to have a balanced, full life without trusting in money. While there are more than 500 verses on prayer and faith, there are 2,000 on the subject of money and possessions. [9] Why does God spend so much time on greed and the dangers of money in His Word? God knows the lure money has for us. Let's look at what the Bible says about how the love of money can dangerously imbalance our Christian lives.

## RICH OR POOR?

Agur in Proverbs 30:8-9 pinpointed the problems of financial imbalance when he said, "Give me neither poverty nor riches, but give me only my daily bread. Otherwise, I may have too much and disown you and say, 'Who is the LORD?' Or I may become poor and steal, and so dishonor the name of my God."

Materialism and greed are not just problems for the rich. The poor can be just as tempted. When some ragged-clothed teens in a rural African village were asked what was the biggest problem among their age group, one answered, "Materialism. People here live only for what they can get – like a new shirt or a radio." [10]

So the lure of money is real for rich and poor. Money itself is not evil; rather, the love of money is the root of all kinds of evil (1 Timothy 6:10). However, money can be used for good.

### The Lord's Work

When the rich young ruler came to Jesus and asked what he should do to have eternal life, he didn't anticipate Jesus' reply. The Lord asked him to sell his possessions, give to the poor, and follow Him. The ruler went away sad because he was rich and was not willing to part with his wealth. After this, Jesus commented to His disciples that it is easier for a camel to go through the eye of a needle than for a rich man to enter the kingdom of God. The Lord knew how difficult it was for people to wave goodbye to their money.

Fortunately, some were more willing to give than to receive (Acts 20:35). Notable examples in the New Testament were the early Jerusalem Christians who shared what they had (2:45; 4:32). The Macedonian churches also gave liberally. Paul tells of them, "Out of the most severe trial, their overflowing joy and their extreme poverty welled up in rich generosity. For I testify that they gave as much as they were able, and even beyond their ability. Entirely on their own, they urgently pleaded with us for the privilege of sharing in this service to the saints. And they did not do as we expected, but they gave themselves first to the Lord and then to us in keeping with God's will" (2 Corinthians 8:2-5). Paul here tells us the key to true giving – giving ourselves first.

While the wealthy gave a portion of their riches to the temple treasury, Jesus commended the widow for giving her last two coins. Was He saying we should give all we have to the church treasury and abandon our other responsibilities? The widow was praised for her generosity in proportion to her livelihood, but we are commanded to fulfill our responsibilities as well.

### Family

The Lord wants us to take care of our families. Timothy encourages older children to repay their parents and grandparents by providing for them, ending with a stern rebuke: "If anyone does not provide for his relatives, and especially for his immediate family, he has denied the faith and is worse than an unbeliever" (5:3-4, 8).

### Government

Jesus did not try to escape taxes but encouraged His followers to give their leaders the tribute they are due (Luke 20:22-25). He even miraculously provided a four-drachma coin for Peter's and His own temple tax (Matthew 17:24-27). If they use them wisely, the government can use funds to improve our lives and protect us.

## MANAGING YOUR MONEY

Christians are to use their money wisely. This principle is vividly taught in Jesus' parable of the shrewd manager. A rich man took his manager to task when the manager was accused of wasting the rich man's possessions. After being fired from his job, the manager knew he would need friends so he canceled part of the debts that the rich man's debtors owed. Although the manager was a rascal, the rich man commended him for his shrewdness.

Then Jesus told His followers that they should also be shrewd with the use of their money. If they cannot be responsible for the little they are stewards of here on earth, how can they be entrusted with real wealth in heaven? We cannot be the slaves of God and money. Slaves must be wholeheartedly devoted to one master. We must be committed to God (Luke 16:1-13). [11]

But how do we prove our commitment to God with our money? Here are some practical ways to honor God with our wealth (Proverbs 3:9-10):

• Make a budget, and strive to balance it. By determining guidelines for certain expenses, you are more likely to control your spending. Ask God to realign your thinking if your wants seem out of balance. Pray about your spending.

• Set aside what you can give to the Lord's work before the bills start coming in and gobbling up your budget. "On the first day of the week, each one of you should set aside a sum of money in keeping with his income, saving it up, so that when I come no collections will have to be made" (1 Corinthians 16:2).

• Give freely to others. "Cast your bread upon the waters, for after many days you will find it again" (Ecclesiastes 11:1). Over and over in God's Word we are taught that generous giving results in abundant blessings. Richard Swenson writes, "God is honored by funnels and dishonored by sponges. Be a conduit of His blessing, not a dead end." [12] Be available to help others when they need it (Proverbs 3:27-28).

• Do not borrow money if possible. "The rich rule over the poor, and the borrower is servant to the lender" (Proverbs 22:7). For some, this may require cutting up the credit cards and spending only what they have. On larger expenses, paying with cash is very difficult. We should try to pay debts back as soon as we can because interest rates are exorbitant. The "buy now, pay later" becomes "binge now, pain later." [13] Benjamin Franklin quipped, "If you would know the value of money, go and try to borrow some."[14]

• Use your money; do not let it use you. God does not forbid us from investing our money wisely. We should pray for wisdom and become informed about the best ways that we can personally use our finances. Learn the most advantageous ways to save your money. Make a will. Do not wait until the death of your spouse or parents to learn about your family finances. John Wesley summed it up well when he said, "Make all you can, save all you can, give all you can." [15]

• Our money is a gift from God; thank Him for it often. "But remember the LORD your God, for it is he who gives you the ability to produce wealth" (Deuteronomy 8:18).

## JUST A LITTLE MORE

Someone asked the millionaire John D. Rockefeller, "How much money is enough?" He replied, "Just a little more."

Sadly, many people in our world are obsessed with getting just a little more. In the process they might lose their health, their families, and their integrity. Money, they believe, is life's report card and they want to make the grade. They spend more but enjoy it less. They might know how to make a living, but not a life. They long for the good life, but only the Lord can make our lives good. They long to be fulfilled, but only He can fill our lives full. Jesus proclaimed, "I have come that they might have life, and have it to the full" (John 10:10).

Paul admonishes,

> Command those who are rich in this present world not to be arrogant nor to put their hope in wealth, which is so uncertain, but to put their hope in God, who richly provides us with everything for our enjoyment. Command them to do good, to be rich in good deeds, and to be generous and willing to share. In this way they will lay up treasure for themselves as a firm foundation for the coming age, so that they may take hold of the life that is truly life (1 Timothy 6:17-19).

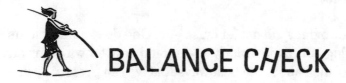

# BALANCE CHECK

*Summarize 2 Corinthians 9:6-11 in your own words.*

1. What are some budget plans you could implement? Which is your favorite?

2. Which wealthy men in these scriptures served God?

   | | |
   |---|---|
   | Genesis 13:2 | Job 1:1-5; 42:12-15 |
   | Genesis 13:5-6 | 2 Chronicles 18:1 |
   | Genesis 26:12-13 | Matthew 27:57 |
   | Genesis 31:14-16 | Luke 19:2 |

3. What is the difference between the attitudes of the man described in Ecclesiastes 4:7-8; 5:16-17 and the man in 5:18-20?

4. What is the portrait of a greedy man described in Proverbs 15:27; 28:25 and 29:4?

5. How was greed connected to the betrayal, crucifixion and resurrection of Jesus? How was liberality connected to the burial of Jesus?

6. How are those who get rich dishonestly described in Proverbs 21:6 and Jeremiah 17:11; 22:13-17?

7. How are the generous man and the stingy man contrasted in these passages: Proverbs 11:24-26; 22:9 and 28:22, 27?

8. Why can't we serve God and money (Matthew 6:24)?

9. What is meant by the statement, "It is not what we give but what we keep that matters"?

10. What do these scriptures say happens to riches: Psalm 49: 16-17; Proverbs 23:5; Matthew 6:19-20; James 5:1-5?

 **TIME OUT**

*"No one is really consecrated until his money is dedicated."* – Roy L. Smith [16]

*"There are no pockets in a shroud."* – Unknown [17]

*"Money used to talk, then it whispered. Now it just sneaks off."* – Unknown [18]

*"The safest way to double your money is to fold it over once and put it in your pocket."* – Kin Hubbard [19]

*"Debt is a trap which a man sets and baits himself – and catches himself."* – Josh Billings [20]

*"Money often costs too much."* – Ralph Waldo Emerson [21]

# CHAPTER 8

# STUFFING YOUR STUFF

*"The best things in life aren't things."*
*– Art Buchwald* [1]

Our lives are full of stuff, aren't they? Listen to what one anonymous writer thought about all her stuff:

Every spring I start sorting my stuff. There is closet stuff, drawer stuff, attic stuff and basement stuff. I separate the good stuff from the bad stuff, then I stuff the bad stuff anywhere the stuff is not too crowded, until I decide if I need the bad stuff.

Whenever we have company, they always bring bags and bags of stuff. When I visit my son, he always moves his stuff so I will have room for my stuff. My daughter-in-law always clears a drawer of her stuff so I will have room for my stuff. It would be so much easier to use their stuff and leave my stuff at home with the rest of my stuff.

I'm thinking of building an extra closet where I would have a place for all the stuff too good to throw away and too bad to keep with my good stuff.

I seem to spend a lot of time with stuff – food stuff, cleaning stuff, medical stuff, clothing stuff and outside stuff. Whatever would life be like if we didn't have all this stuff?

There is stuff to make us smell better, stuff to make our hair look good, stuff to make us look younger, stuff to make us look healthier, stuff to play with, stuff to entertain us and stuff to eat.

We stuff ourselves with the food stuff.

When the Lord calls me home, my children will want the good stuff but the bad stuff – stuffed wherever there is room among all the other stuff – will be stuffed in bags and taken to the dump where all the other people's stuff has been taken.

Our lives are filled with stuff – good stuff, bad stuff, little stuff, big stuff, useful stuff, junky stuff and assorted stuff. When we leave all our stuff and go to heaven, it won't matter what happens to our stuff. We'll get the good stuff God has waiting for us and there won't be any more sorting stuff. [2]

In Luke 12:16-21, a farmer had a problem with his stuff. His harvest was so bountiful, he didn't know what to do with it. His bumper crop filled all his existing barns. He decided to tear down his barns and build bigger ones to accommodate the overflow and then take it easy and live off the fat of his land. But God told him that that very night his life would be demanded of him. Then who would enjoy his wealth?

This farmer had so much that he didn't know where to stuff his stuff. This malady isn't unique to rich, productive farmers in Palestine. We in America also have too much and don't know where to put it.

It wasn't wrong for the farmer to have a profitable harvest or to be rich. He just didn't want to let go of his possessions. Sometimes neither do we. When we cram one more dress in our overcrowded closets or relegate one more unused gadget to our garages or hide one more piece of junk in our attics, are we not hoarding things like the farmer?

In this parable of the rich farmer, Jesus was not recommending that we all should spend the rest of our lives in one-room apartments even if we are running out of room. He was not condemning making adequate space for legitimate reasons – more people in the family, for instance. Neither is He criticizing preparation for the future. He is asking if we need to keep everything we are blessed with. Are we always building bigger and better barns for our wealth while the rest of the world suffers in poverty and sin? The farmer was condemned for his poverty toward God. His overconfidence in his riches and himself overshadowed his reliance on God.

Later in Luke 12, Jesus tells us why holding on to our stuff gets in the way of balance in our lives.

• Hoarding things makes us worry about our stuff too much. The more we have, the more we have to repair, oil, trim, mow, shine, vacuum, wash, dry, clean, mop and dust! Our time, money and energy can be consumed by our possessions (Luke 12:22-30). We need to realize where our treasures really are (Matthew 6:19-20).

• Hoarding things can keep us from sharing with others. If our heartstrings are bound by things, they are not free to give. But a generous heart reaps eternal treasure. "Sell your possessions and give to the poor. Provide purses for yourselves that will not wear out, a treasure in heaven that will not be exhausted, where no thief comes near and no moth destroys. For where you treasure is, there your heart will be also" (Luke 12:33-34).

• Hoarding things can keep us from focusing on seeking the kingdom. If we seek God's kingdom first, our necessities like food and clothes will be supplied (Luke 12:31).

You might ask, but what does all this have to do with me? Just because my closet or garage or attic is overflowing doesn't mean I'm greedy. Or does it?

Do we need all we have? Could some of our still usable things be used by someone else? Should some unusable things that clutter our homes and our lives just be thrown away? One visit to a developing country will graphically demonstrate to us how basic our needs really are. As Paul states, "But if we have food, and clothing, we will be content with that" (1 Timothy 6:8). Can we really learn to be content with less?

We could learn much from our Grandma's sampler about being content and stretching what we have. One heirloom was stitched: "Use it up, Wear it out, Make it do, Do without." Of course, this can be taken to extremes. It is sometimes more economical to buy new stuff than fix the old. But often we are too eager to throw out the old and bring in the new before the old is used up. Learning to garden, sew, barter, recycle and make handmade gifts are just a few of the ways to make what we have go a little further.

## OVERCOMING AFFLUENZA

In this materialistic society, we often catch "affluenza," the desire to always want more and more. Unfortunately, affluenza is spreading in epidemic proportions! We look at others and can always find someone with a newer car, a fancier house or more fashionable clothes than ours. But the wise man in Ecclesiastes 4:6 states, "Better one handful with tranquility than two handfuls with toil and chasing after the wind." It is better to have peace and happiness with less than to work ourselves to death to be richer. Paul echoes this thought in Philippians 4:6-7: "Do not be anxious about anything, but in everything, by prayer and petition, with thanksgiving, present your requests to God. And the peace of God, which transcends all understanding, will guard your hearts and your minds in Christ Jesus."

How can we achieve this contentment? The writer of Hebrews gives the answer:

> Keep your lives free from the love of money and be content with what you have, because God has said, "Never will I leave you; never will I forsake you." So we say with confidence, "The Lord is my helper; I will not be afraid. What can man do to me?" (Hebrews 13:5-6).

With assurance like that, we can put our confidence in God and not in things. We can truly feel content in the Lord. Paul reaches the same conclusion in Philippians 4:11-13:

> [F]or I have learned to be content whatever the circumstances. I know what it is to be in need, and I know

what it is to have plenty. I have learned the secret of being content in any and every situation, whether well fed or hungry, whether living in plenty or in want. I can do everything through him who gives me strength.

G.K. Chesterton pointed out, "There are two ways to get enough. One is to continue to accumulate more and more. The other is to desire less." [3] We can learn to be content with the stuff we have. But some Stuff Stuffers can't seem to stuff enough.

## MEET THE STUFF STUFFERS

Let's meet some bona fide members of the Stuff Stuffers. Stuff seems to be stuffed into their houses and spills into the garage, attic, utility buildings … .

• Pack-Rat Patty keeps everything in case she might need it someday. Some of the stuff is yellowing or moth-eaten in her drawers and closets, but she is still saving it for a special occasion. Just because she hasn't used or needed these things in 30 years does not deter her from her purpose.

• Hideaway Hilda might not keep it all, but what she keeps is stashed away. She's trying to hide the stuff from thieves. There is only one problem – she can't find it herself!

• Cluttered Claudia doesn't worry about stashing it away – it is cluttered everywhere. If a messy home is happy, then hers is delirious. Her motto: A place for everything and everything all over the place.

Perhaps you see yourself in one or all of these women. Is there an answer to the stuffing dilemma?

Paul wrote, "But everything should be done in a fitting and orderly way" (1 Corinthians 14:40). Although this was written in the context of disorderly worship, it certainly is appropriate for every facet of our lives. Our God is a God of beauty and order, and He wants us to be more like Him. We can concentrate more on the spiritual in our lives if we become more disciplined in our physical lives. We must admit that an orderly home makes life easier. We do not have to be uncomfortably rigid about order, but we don't have to become House Hogs either! If we have a place to put our

keys, socks and driver's license, we don't have to spend time,
energy and money looking for them. Remember how Jesus fed
the 5,000 with five loaves of bread and two fish? He had the disciples seat the people in groups of 50 and when everyone was finished eating, they gathered the leftovers (Luke 9:14-17). This shows
us how Jesus saw the value of being orderly and making the most
of what was available.

## CUTTING THE CLUTTER

We can find balance in stuffing our stuff by cutting the clutter.
We can begin by using little swatches of time to implement the
"salami technique." By cutting something big into smaller slices
(like 15-30 minute time bites), you can avoid getting bogged down
and will be surprised what you can accomplish. Start with an easy
drawer or small closet. If the project still seems overwhelming,
ask a clutter buddy to help you and give you moral support.

• Analyze what you have and what you really need. What works
for your situation, and what doesn't? Do we own some things we
don't need or use just to impress others? Go through your stuff, and
cull what doesn't belong. You can sort items into three categories:

1. Keepers. Stuff you enjoy and want to keep.
2. Sleepers. Stuff that needs to be repaired or updated
   before it will be usable, like a dress with a loose hem
   or a kitchen appliance that needs to be fixed.
3. Heapers. Stuff that we cannot use or do not want, like
   clothes that don't fit or a lawn mower that cannot be
   repaired. Either we should sell the things, find someone to use them, or throw them away. Someone might
   be able to use something we cannot. If you are uncertain whether to get rid of something, box it up out
   of sight and wait six months. If you don't miss it, you
   probably don't need it. Whenever you buy something
   new, get rid of something old.

• Prioritize your mail. Sort your mail in these categories: to read,
to pay, to do, to file. Act on it as soon as you can. Recycle or throw
away the junk mail.

• Utilize all the space you have for storage. About 10 percent of our home is needed for storing our stuff. Deniece Schofield quips, "Remember the law of the home: Junk expands to fill the space available, plus one room." [4]

• Methodize. Make it a habit to always put your glasses, keys, purse, watch and other important objects in certain places so you will always be able to find them. If you spend 10 minutes a day looking for misplaced items, in a year that would total more than 60 hours! [5]

## GOD'S PERSPECTIVE

Eliminating clutter will bring us well on our way to stuffing our stuff in a way that would be pleasing to God. We need to get a fresh perspective, a new appreciation for our blessings – the way God looks at stuff.

One father tried to get this across to his son. The father hoped his son would better appreciate his blessings when he saw first-hand what it meant to live with less. So the family went to visit their underprivileged friends on a small farm. When they got home, he asked his son if he understood better what it meant to be poor.

"I sure do!" his son replied. "We have one dog, and they have five. We have a swimming pool in the back yard, and they have a creek that never ends. We have a car, and they get to ride horses. Thanks, Dad, for showing me how poor we really are!" [6]

Looking through God's perspective helps us see who all our stuff really belongs to. "Every good and perfect gift is from above, coming down from the Father of the heavenly lights, who does not change like shifting shadows" (James 1:17). All our stuff is really on loan from God; it is up to us to use it for Him. Our possessions can be used to glorify Him and honor His name. Or they can be used to bring a wedge between God and us. We decide. Possessions aren't a problem unless they possess us.

# BALANCE CHECK

*Summarize Ecclesiastes 5:10-16 in your own words.*

1. In the parallel passages James 1:22, 27 and 1 John 3:17-18, what do James and John write that we should go beyond in providing for others?
2. Who really owns our possessions (Psalm 24:1; 1 Chronicles 29:14; Haggai 2:8)?
3. How did the rich men in these scriptures use their possessions?

   1 Samuel 25:2

   2 Samuel 19:32

   1 Kings 10: 23-29

   2 Chronicles 18:1

   2 Chronicles 32:27

   Luke 16:19

4. What is necessary whenever we give to others or to God (1 Corinthians 13:3)?
5. How can Christians have nothing, yet possess all things (1 Corinthians 6:10)?
6. On what should our minds be set (Colossians 3:2)?
7. What is the difference between the world Jesus loved (John 3:16) and the world we should not love (1 John 2:15-17)?
8. How can our stuff impair our balance in life (Luke 12:22-34)?
9. What was Paul's secret to contentment (Philippians 4:11-13)?
10. Why did the men in Matthew 13:44-46 sell all their possessions? What do these parables mean?

 # TIME OUT

*"The happiest people don't necessarily have the best of everything. They just make the best of everything." – Unknown* [7]

*"If your riches are yours, why don't you take them with you to the other world?" – Benjamin Franklin* [8]

*"The goods we spend we keep; and what we save we lose; and only what we lose we have." – Francis Quarles* [9]

*"Every increased possession loads us with a new weariness." – John Ruskin* [10]

*"Who lives content with little possesses everything." – Nicolas Boileau* [11]

*"The wise man carries his possessions within him." – Bias* [12]

## CHAPTER 9

# GIVING YOUR GIFTS BACK

*"God has a slot in his total eternal plan for each of us.
That slot is exactly the shape of our heritage, experience
and life, and He expects us to fill it."*
*— Sarah Gudschinsky* [1]

Louella Smiddy or "Mama Lou," as she was affectionately known, had a gift for teaching. Beginning at the age of 16, she taught school and continued to teach until she retired. In her later years, she had a wish to live out the rest of her life as a missionary in Ecuador where the high altitudes made her feel closer to heaven.

Mama Lou got her wish. Her last 10 years were spent with her daughter in Ecuador, where Mama Lou helped the Christians there with her optimistic counsel and wit.

It isn't unheard of for a missionary to die in his or her country of service. What is so remarkable about Mama Lou Smiddy was her age when she died — 103! At her funeral, the mile-long procession was made up of Mestizos, Indians, Americans and Europeans who honored her memory and her gift. [2]

We might not be able to enjoy Mama Lou's longevity of life, but we can certainly emulate her spirit — her joy in giving back the gifts that she had received of God. Part of our purpose in life is discovering our God-given gifts and giving them back to God. As someone has said, "What you are is God's gift to you; what you make of yourself is your gift to God." [3]

# DIFFERENT GIFTS

What are our gifts or talents? A gift is something you are good at, something that makes you feel like you have made a contribution, and usually something you enjoy doing. Is there something you enjoy doing, even when you were a child? Do others consistently compliment you on a specific ability? This gift you have can be used by God in His kingdom.

Paul reminded the Romans that, just as the human body has many members with various roles to play, so the church is made up of many members with different functions. "We have different gifts, according to the grace given us" (Romans 12:6). Then he enumerates several gifts – serving, teaching, encouraging, giving, leading and showing mercy. (Miraculous spiritual gifts like prophesying and healing were needed at that time, but are not needed now with God's full revelation.)

In 1 Corinthians 12, Paul emphasized that every part of the body, or church, is important and that the gifts are equally valuable. With different gifts being utilized by various members, we can see how God foresaw a balance of talent in the church. There was no need for feelings of superiority or inadequacy because everyone's talent could be used and appreciated.

> But God has combined the members of the body and
> has given greater honor to the parts that lacked it, so
> that there should be no division in the body, but that
> its parts should have equal concern for each other
> (1 Corinthians 12:24-25).

How are gifts to be used? Peter tells us in 1 Peter 4:10: "Each one should use whatever gift he has received to serve others, faithfully administering God's grace in its various forms." God will freely give His children gifts, but it is up to them to learn how to use them for His glory. Unfortunately, our gifts do not come gift-wrapped with instructions. We are like 10-speed bikes – we have several gears we never use! [4] Our challenge is first to discover what our gifts are and then to use them, not lose them, as illustrated in a story Jesus told.

# USE THEM OR LOSE THEM

In Matthew 25:14-30, Jesus told the parable of the talents in which a master gave one servant five talents, another servant two, and the third servant one. A talent was a sum of money worth more than $1,000, so it was quite a responsibility the master bestowed on his servants. The first two servants doubled their money and received the master's praise. Note that those two received the exact commendation even though they had a different number of talents. The crucial thing was not the number of their talents but what they did with them. The one-talent man was condemned. Was it because he only had one talent? No, it was because he did nothing with what he had. His talent was taken away and given to the 10-talent man.

Likewise, we will be condemned if we bury our talents. If we fail to discover what we can do for God, untapped reservoirs of service will be lost. God won't ask us why we were not more like someone else but rather how we fulfilled our own potential. In utilizing our gifts to the fullest, we can fulfill His plan for us. It is truly awesome to think that God has a special plan for each one of us. S.C. McAuley said, "God made you as you are in order to use you as he planned." [5]

To fulfill God's purpose for our lives, we must first discern His will through prayer, worship and Bible study. No matter what we feel our purpose is, it must be aligned with God's will. Only in God can we reach our full potential.

We also need to understand our individual natures to fulfill our purpose. God made us all different – shy or talkative, emotional or intellectual, well organized or spontaneous. The world is much more interesting that way. But more important, there is a place for every temperament. Think of Peter – impetuous, yet a courageous spokesman for the apostles. Where would the early church have been without him? But what if every apostle had been like Peter? The church also needed men like the evangelist Philip, the encourager Barnabas and the physician Luke.

Consider Priscilla, Lydia and Dorcas – these women were active in using their gifts within their circumstances. Priscilla shared the work of making tents and teaching Apollos with her husband Aquila.

Lydia, a dealer in purple cloth and probably a wealthy woman, opened her heart to God's message and opened her home to Paul and his fellow travelers. Dorcas must have been a busy seamstress, for the poor widows showed Peter the robes and other clothing she had made for them. All these women used the resources they had, and so should we. Whether we are single or married, rich, poor or in between, we can use our gifts to fulfill God's purpose.

Working within God's will and our individual natures in our circumstances, we can utilize the gifts that God has blessed us with to their fullest. Wherever your talent lies, there is a place for it in God's kingdom. [6] As Mordecai asked Esther, "Who knoweth whether thou art come to the kingdom for such a time as this? (Esther 4:14 KJV). Miriam Adeney writes,

> Ask yourself, What have I come to the kingdom for? What gifts, friendships, dreams do I have that are unique? What will not get done in this world unless I do it (besides scrubbing my kitchen table)? ... Because God has empowered us, our work is serious, whatever it is. We are not jacks-of-all-trades-masters-of-none. That's a trap we women easily can fall into. Our diffuse responsibilities can water down our focus. ... We are each uniquely and differently gifted. That's no light matter. [7]

## DEDICATING OUR GIFTS

Whether we work inside or outside the home, our gifts can be used to God's glory. Paul wrote, "And whatever you do, whether in word or deed, do it all in the name of the Lord Jesus, giving thanks to God the Father through him" (Colossians 3:17 NIV). Any task, whether great or small, can be dedicated to Him.

When we dedicate our efforts to God, does that mean that we must do everything perfectly? God doesn't ask for perfect work or impossible standards. However, that doesn't justify inferior workmanship or laziness either. Can you imagine Jesus turning out shoddy carpentry work? There is a balance between perfectionism and slovenliness and that is to do our best. The baseball great

Orel Hershiser wrote, "To call myself a Christian and then not strive to be the best I can be and do the most I can with what has been given me would be the height of hypocrisy. Being a Christian is no excuse for mediocrity." [8]

God asks the best of us. What if we do our best, but don't receive the appreciation we feel we deserve for our hard work? Paul reminded Christian slaves of the One to work for and please. The same holds true for Christian workers today:

> Slaves, obey your earthly masters in everything; and do it, not only when their eye is on you and to win their favor, but with sincerity of heart and reverence for the Lord. Whatever you do, work at it with all your heart, as working for the Lord, not for men, since you know that you will receive an inheritance from the Lord as a reward. It is the Lord Christ you are serving (Colossians 3:22-24).

We serve God ultimately by giving our gifts back to Him. Our gifts go full circle – God blesses us with them, and we give them back to Him.

## DO WHAT YOU CAN

But someone might say, "I'm only a one-half talent woman! I can't do much – I'm just not talented." Often talent can be developed from hard work and dedication. There will be certain things that we can do better than others, while they will excel in areas where we lack. Why despair and complain about talents in which we are not skilled? We should focus on our strengths and develop them for God's service.

A single Christian lady had always wanted to be a missionary to a foreign country. Her heart was in spreading the Gospel in this way, but her health prevented her from going. She determined that she would use the gifts she had to help missionaries who were already there. She wrote them letters, sent them care packages of items they missed, sewed clothes for them, supported them financially, and even encouraged others to join them on a full-time or short-term basis. Those missionaries were ever thankful for her gifts. Jesus said, "And if anyone gives even a cup of cold water to one of these little ones because he is my disciple, I tell you the truth, he will certainly not lose his reward" (Matthew 10:42). No act of service, no use of one's gift, is too insignificant.

What are some ways to help one another develop our gifts? Compliment others when they excel at something. Hold classes and workshops to develop new talents like teaching or sewing. Share a skill with a younger person like baking bread or crocheting. Co-teach with another Christian to learn from each other. Try something you have never done before like visiting a prison or going on a Bible study (but do your homework first). Encourage someone who is hesitant to serve by helping her prepare or by going with her. Create new avenues of service and involvement by finding out what gifts the ladies of the congregation possess and brainstorm how these gifts can best be used. Can some artist help with teaching visuals or bulletin boards? Can a doctor, dentist or nurse be supported in a long-term or short-term medical effort? Can an author write articles for the church bulletin, Bible curriculum or brotherhood publications?

When you are doing what you really enjoy, you often do it well. But when it is used for God, it takes on greater meaning and blessing. When you discover your gifts and use them for God, you will find true happiness and joy. Denise Turner wrote, "Think seriously about what gives you the greatest joy in life ... and then build on that. Perhaps you can work it into a hobby, or an occupation, or a family activity; but build it into your life wherever possible, as fully as possible, as often as possible. For, when you have found the thing that gives you joy, you have found what you were truly created to do." [9]

# BALANCE CHECK

*Summarize Romans 12:3-8 in your own words.*

1. How did Peter say our gifts should be used (1 Peter 4:10)?

2. In the parable of the talents, why were the two servants commended and the one servant condemned? What happened to the talents their master gave them?

3. What are the different gifts listed in Romans 12:6-8? Why are some of these gifts not needed today?

4. How did Paul compare the different parts of the body to members of the church with different gifts (1 Corinthians 12:12-31)?

5. How did Esther, Priscilla, Lydia and Dorcas use their gifts for God?

6. How can we determine what God's specific purpose is in using our gifts?

7. How can we better develop our gifts?

8. What are some ways we can encourage each other in developing our gifts?

9. What principles given in these scriptures – Romans 12:18; Ephesians 6:5-9; Colossians 3:22-25; 4:1; 2 Thessalonians 3:10; 1 Timothy 6:1-2; Titus 2:9-10; 1 Peter 2:18-22 – could apply to work situations today?

10. In these scriptures, how does the writer in Proverbs relate laziness to poverty: Proverbs 6:9-11; 10:4; 14:23; 20:13: 21:17; 24:33-34; 28:19?

 # TIME OUT

*"Doing your best is more important than being the best."* – *Unknown* [10]

*"Don't measure yourself by what you have accomplished, but what you should have accomplished with your ability."* – *John Wesley* [11]

*"Better be proficient in one art than a smatterer in a hundred."* – *Japanese Proverb* [12]

*"You have been blessed with special skills that are yours alone. Use them, whatever they may be, and forget about wearing another's hat."* – *Og Mandino* [13]

*"To find out what one is fitted to do and to secure an opportunity to do it is the key to happiness."* – *John Dewey* [14]

*"Be not simply good; be good for something."* – *Henry David Thoreau* [15]

## CHAPTER 10

# RUNNING ON EMPTY

*"The graveyards are full of women whose houses
were so spotless you could eat off the floor."*
*– Heloise Cruse* [1]

D rained. Exhausted. Depleted. These words are not describing oil reserves, natural resources or bank funds. They describe people – the most valuable resource of all – when they have given and given and feel they cannot give any more. They feel like they are running on empty.

Women are prime candidates for this hollow condition. Often givers by nature, we try to take care of everyone else's needs while our own needs are sometimes neglected. With people and projects demanding our attention, we try to fulfill our responsibilities to our families, church, work and community. Sometimes all these responsibilities leave us ready to crash and burnout.

Only by filling our own cups will we have something left to fill the cups of others. Only by achieving an emotional and spiritual personal balance can we be of service to anyone else. It's just like the informational speech of the flight attendant at the beginning of each flight. In a low oxygen emergency, we must first put an oxygen mask over our mouths and noses before we can assist a child. We must preserve and maintain our well-being before we can help anyone else. God knew that and even sanctioned rest.

## EVEN GOD RESTED

God thought it was important to rest: "And God blessed the seventh day and made it holy, because on it he rested from all the work of creating that he had done" (Genesis 2:3). God did not have to rest. He is all-powerful and does not have to sleep. But He instituted the Sabbath as a day for the Israelites to refuel and refocus on spiritual things.

No doubt, Israelite families needed a day of rest. After traveling through the desert and working in an arid climate, they needed a time to rejuvenate their bodies and souls. God did not create the human body to go nonstop, so He instituted a mandatory break, a forced rest.

God was serious about this day of rest. Not only were the Israelites to observe the Sabbath, but also any livestock, slaves and aliens with them were to observe it (Exodus 20:8-11). They were to observe it during even the busiest times of plowing season and harvest. The penalty for disobedience was death.

If rest was important enough to God, then it has a place in our lives as well. But our culture is not one to sit still. It is not easy for many people to take it easy. It is hard work for them to pamper themselves.

## PUSHING FAST FORWARD

Do you ever feel like a videotape turned on fast forward? You are going through life so fast you don't have time to savor the present or prepare for the future.

Your body cannot continue in this revved up state for long. It starts to break down just like a tape does after extended use. Our bodies show signs of wear with exhaustion, heart disease, gastric problems, hypertension, depression and many other ailments.

In the last two decades, stress-related diseases have mushroomed among women. With a third of Americans saying that they feel rushed to do the things they have to do, we can see why. Ironically, the time we need to relax the most is when we don't have time for it. Stress is actually a necessary part of our lives, but we have to find a healthy balance between too much and too little.

Dr. Howard Rusk said, "Stress is really an integral part of life. We set our whole pattern of life by our stress end-point. If we hit it exactly, we live dynamic, purposeful, useful, happy lives. If we go over, we break. If we stay too far under, we vegetate." [2]

To achieve balance, we cannot always operate in overdrive. Sometimes we just need to pause in our busy lives and take a breather. Dorothy Ballard said, "Learn to pause – or nothing worthwhile will catch up with you." [3] Instead of pushing fast forward, we can learn to push pause. Let's look at some ways to slow down and refocus.

## PUSHING PAUSE

• Laugh. It has been reported that 5-year-olds laugh an average of 113 times a day, while 44-year-olds laugh only about 11 times a day. In the intervening years, what happens to the chuckle factor? [4] Proverbs 17:22 states, "A cheerful heart is good medicine, but a crushed spirit dries up the bones." Humor can be like medicine, but it costs less and tastes better! It's true that life is not always humorous, but it certainly helps if we can make some of it fun. Spend time with people who see the bright side of life. Keep a file of funny cartoons and stories to bring out when you are feeling blue. Watch a funny video. Lighten up! [5]

• Learn to relax. We all look forward to the weekend to do what? Take a trip? Start a new hobby? Fly kites with the kids? Catch up on the housework? The choice is ours. One poll found that while 95 percent of working mothers eagerly anticipated the weekend, 52 percent felt exhausted when it was over. [6]

Similarly, vacations are a joke to some people. They schedule each minute and feel guilty if they sit still. They come home more tired than when they started. As someone has quipped, "No man needs a vacation so much as the man who has just had one." We should be sure our vacations are real breaks from our normal activities so that we can come back refreshed and restored.

God commanded that every seventh year the fields of the Israelites should be fallow and untilled (Exodus 23:10-12). What a good idea for our bodies and spirits – just to rest and relax

occasionally! Yet many people feel guilty when they relax. All of a
Christian's time is worthwhile. He doesn't have to separate it into
"important work time" and "frivolous free time." It's all important
to God and belongs to Him. It can all be used for His service. There
is a definite place for leisure time. Tim Hansel says,

> We have yet to learn that true leisure is not idleness, and
> that leisure is each man's touchstone with himself and
> his inner resources. We haven't yet decided how much
> value to give to the leisure in our lives. As a result we
> don't know how to put it in a proper balance with work.[7]

Balancing work and leisure is a challenge for all of us. We don't
have to feel guilty when we occasionally take time for ourselves.

• Sleep. Sociologist Arlie Hochschild found some mothers were
so exhausted that they talked about sleep like a hungry person
talks about food. They describe themselves as "bone-weary,"
"ragged," "busy every waking hour," and "sinking in quicksand."
Sleep has become a casualty of modern life. [8]

Some people need more sleep as they get older; some need less.
Be sure you are getting what you need. For most adults, that's
about eight hours. Sleep is important for renewing brain struc-
tures, repairing worn-out tissues, and releasing growth hormones.
Without sleep, we are more prone to illness, accidents and low
productivity. Annually "springing forward" for daylight savings
time and losing an hour of sleep causes a 7 percent increase in
that day's traffic accidents! [9]

Our relationship with God can affect our sleep. One woman, ex-
periencing great trials in her life, was still able to sleep peacefully. When asked her secret, she replied, "I've handed my life and
my problems to the Lord. Since He never slumbers or sleeps, there
is no use both of us should stay awake!"

Even short naps can refresh us. However, we shouldn't nap too
long or it might interfere with our evening rest. During World War
II, Winston Churchill was able to work through the night until the
early morning because he insisted on an afternoon nap. Other fa-
mous nappers include Anwar Sadat, Napoleon, Thomas Edison
and Harry Truman. [10]

• Take care of your body. It has been said that after the age of 40, our bodies are like inner tubes – they need to be patched and repaired! Having regular checkups with the doctor, drinking plenty of water, eating right, taking supplements if needed – all these contribute to our overall well-being. God values us and wants us to take care of ourselves.

> Do you not know that your body is a temple of the Holy Spirit, who is in you, whom you have received from God? You are not your own, you were bought at a price. Therefore honor God with your body (1 Corinthians 6:19-20).

We honor God by maintaining the body He gave us. Izaak Walton said, "Look to your health, and if you have it, praise God, and value it next to a good conscience; for health is the second blessing that we mortals are capable of; a blessing that money cannot buy." Treat yourself well – you are one of the best friends you have! [11]

• Get moving. Find ways to be more active. Reasonably active people are at less risk than sedentary people for diabetes, high blood pressure, stress, obesity and some forms of cancer. Get involved in group sports, or strike out on your own. You don't have to be a marathon runner to benefit from movement. Research shows that any activity, regardless of how intense or long can produce worthwhile results. Taking the stairs, walking wherever you can, talking to a neighbor face-to-face instead of by phone – all these help keep us active.

• Socialize. Factor time into your schedule for maintaining relationships just like other commitments. Take a few minutes for a phone call or short visit with a neighbor. Find common times you can get together – breakfast might work as well as a girl's night out.

For more balance, include different types of people in your life. Various people affect us differently – some drain us, some refresh us, and some affect us neutrally. People need us to help and encourage them. Although we should try to nourish everyone we can, we need to spend time with the people who can nourish and replenish us as well. Invest more of yourself in two-way friendships. Jesus ministered to the multitude but found deeper friendships in the Twelve and even closer kinship with Peter, James and John. [12]

• Refill your inner cup. Discover what you really enjoy, and make the time to do it. Maybe it is gardening, writing, working with children or the elderly – doing something totally different from what you do every day. Learn something new. Escape from your rut, and change your pace and outlook. It can invigorate you.

## JESUS OFFERS REST

Although He lived before the age of pollution, road rage and school shootings, Christ understood weariness in His followers and offered them a chance for relief. In Mark 6:30-32, His apostles had just returned to report to Jesus all they had done and taught. Probably exhausted already from their travels, they longed for a breather just to have some time alone with the Lord to get His feedback on everything that had happened. Jesus sensed this, but the crowds wanted to see Jesus at the same time. Verses 31-32 say, "Then, because so many people were coming and going that they did not even have a chance to eat, he said to them, 'Come with me by yourselves to a quiet place and get some rest.' So they went away by themselves in a boat to a solitary place." The solitude did not last long because the crowds still followed them there. But Jesus recognized that His chosen ones needed a reprieve from the cares of the world.

David said, "My soul finds rest in God alone; my salvation comes from him" (Psalm 62:1). Jesus offers us a retreat from the world of stress and strain. He invites us to rest even today. Only in Him can we be refueled and refilled when we are running on empty.

# BALANCE CHECK

*Summarize Matthew 11:28-30 in your own words.*

1. Why did God institute the Sabbath for the Israelites, and how did He enforce its observance (Genesis 2:3; Exodus 20:8-11; 31:12-17)?

2. What different meanings does the word "rest" have in these scriptures: Joshua 14:15; 2 Samuel 7:12; 1 Chronicles 28:2?

3. Who slept when they should have been praying (Matthew 26:45)?

4. How did a man break the Sabbath, and how was he punished (Numbers 15:32-36)?

5. What precautions did Nehemiah take to prevent the Jews in Jerusalem from buying and selling on the Sabbath (Nehemiah 13:15-22)?

6. What happened while the people in the scriptures listed were sleeping?

    Genesis 2:21                    Genesis 28:10-15

    Genesis 41:1 7                  Judges 4:21

    Judges 16:19-20                 1 Samuel 26:12

    Jonah 1:5                       Matthew 8:24

    Acts 20:9

7. In these scriptures – Esther 6:1 and Daniel 2:1 – what resulted when these people could not sleep?

8. What do you think H.W. Beecher meant when he said, "A man without mirth is like a wagon without springs; he is jolted disagreeably by every pebble in the road"?

9. What are some ways that stress takes its toll on us physically and emotionally?

10. What are some ways we can refuel ourselves?

 # TIME OUT

*"Life is not merely being alive, but being well."*
*— Martial* [13]

*"Leisure nourishes the body and the mind."*
*— Ovid* [14]

*"He sows hurry and reaps indigestion." — Robert*
*Louis Stevenson* [15]

*"Our body is a well-set clock, which keeps good*
*time, but if it be too much or indiscreetly tam-*
*pered with, the alarm runs out before the hour."*
*— Joseph Hall* [16]

*"Laughter is the purest form of our response to*
*God's acceptance of us. For when I laugh at myself,*
*I accept myself." — H.A. Williams* [17]

*"Men tire themselves in pursuit of rest." — Laurence*
*Sterne* [18]

CHAPTER 11

# MEETING YOUR BEST FRIEND

*"God often visits us, but most of the time
we are not at home." – Joseph Roux* [1]

Best friends – they laugh together, cry together and listen to each other. They are always there when they are needed. They share good times and bad. They keep in touch. Their friendship is precious. They are almost like family.

As Christians, we have a Best Friend. He is ready to listen and talk at any time. He is always available. He is never too busy or sick, and He always understands. He has written us reams of letters, but sometimes He doesn't hear from us very much.

How do we meet God, our Best Friend? God communicates to us through His Word. We talk to Him through prayer. Through these avenues, we meet our Best Friend.

With our loud, hectic lives, getting together is not always easy. We first have to slow down and be still. "Be still, and know that I am God" (Psalm 46:10). When the Lord passed by Elijah, He was not in the powerful wind, the shattering earthquake, or the raging fire, but in a gentle whisper (1 Kings 19:11-12). Our all-powerful God is also very approachable. He is always ready to listen. How ready are we?

# A LAMP TO MY FEET

Meeting a friend usually doesn't happen by accident. We plan for it and make the time because it is important. It's just as important to set aside some time for God. We need to know what God is saying to us, or our relationship will go sour. It won't happen unless we designate a block of time. For some women with sporadic schedules, like new mothers, care givers, or women on different work shifts, this block of time might change every day.

There are many different but effective ways to approach the Bible, and we can balance our study by using these various methods. If you haven't read the Bible through, you might find if helpful to find a schedule to read it through in a year. F. LaGard Smith provides interesting commentary in the chronological *Daily Bible*, which is divided into 365 daily readings.

Topical, chapter and book studies give a general overall understanding, while emphasis on verses or keywords gives a more in-depth view. Studies on the men and women of the Bible give us examples of how to live our lives. The life of Christ is especially beneficial if harmonies are used. Other interesting studies include the Psalms, the Proverbs and the prophets.

Some women take their study a step further and combine devotional thoughts, a song, scripture and prayer. Devotional guides such as *Power for Today* and the center section of *Christian Woman* are ideal for this purpose. Others write their spiritual insights in journals. They see how their prayers are answered by dating requests and answers.

Memorization can be a part of devotional time or interspersed throughout the day. Using cards, some new mothers put Bible verses over the changing table. Other women use recipe holders in the kitchen where they wash dishes or tape a card to the mirror over the bathroom sink. Listening to tapes as we drive or do our housework can help us saturate our minds with the Word.

A simple mnemonic, BEAMS (see figure 3), can help us keep our focus in Bible study.

FIGURE 3

**B**ackground – Who wrote it? Who was it written to?
When, where and why was it written?
**E**xplanation  –  What did it mean then? What does it mean now?
**A**pplication  –  How can I apply it?
**M**emory  –  Can some part of it be committed to memory?
**S**hare  –  How can I share it with someone?

We never know when we will be called upon to share those verses we have memorized and put in our hearts. A lady had memorized Acts 2:38 and knew how it could save her. One day a thief snatched her handbag and she strained to remember the verse that could save her. She finally screamed, "Acts 2:38!" On hearing that, the thief threw down her purse and took off around the corner, only to bump headlong into the police. When they later questioned why he dropped the purse, he replied, "What was I to do – she had an axe and two thirty-eights!"

Psalm 119:105 tells us, "Your word is a lamp to my feet and a light for my path." In the time of Jesus, men did not have flashlights to see in the dark. They used tiny lamps with oil that would not slosh out and strapped them to their shoes. The light beams would shine in the dark just enough to light their way home. So it is with God's Word. It can shed God's glorious light in this dark world of sin and help us find our way home. [2]

# TEACH US TO PRAY

Friends do not exist long in a one-sided relationship. They need to talk as well as listen. Jesus talked with His disciples as they traveled and ate, and they often asked Him questions. One question was especially unusual.

Jesus' disciples had no doubt been taught from the Law to pray from an early age. Yet in Jesus, they saw a genuine, dynamic prayer life. No wonder they said, "Lord, teach us to pray" (Luke 11:1). Instead of explaining the elements of a perfect prayer, He just prayed. He demonstrated in the Lord's Prayer that even though a prayer might be simple and short it could be eloquent and powerful.

Throughout His ministry, He taught about the importance of prayer as a communion with the Father. His life was evidence of this close relationship. Though they were separated, Father and Son were always in touch through prayer. Otto Borchert wrote,

> Prayer went like a divine shuttle backwards and forwards between Him and the Father – speech and answer, giving and receiving, a continual loving aloud, in the most intimate tones that the world has ever heard.[3]

Prayer was an integral part of the short three-year ministry of Jesus. Jesus prayed often, sometimes getting up early in the morning or spending the entire night in prayer (Mark 1:35; Luke 6:12). But someone might say, Jesus did not live a hectic life like we do. He did not have a wife or kids, or punch a time clock. Let's look at a day in the life of Jesus.

In Matthew 14:13, Jesus heard about the tragic death of John the Baptist at the hands of Herod. The Lord privately withdrew in a boat, no doubt to mourn His cousin. But the crowds found Him, and He compassionately healed them. With evening coming and the people getting hungry, He fed more than 5,000 people. Afterward He sent the disciples ahead in a boat and dismissed the crowd while He went into the hills to pray alone again.

During the fourth watch of the night (between 3 and 6 a.m.), Jesus walked on the lake to get to the disciples in the boat. They were terrified, thinking He was a ghost. When He had convinced them, Peter was eager to try walking on the water himself. He almost walked to Jesus but then faltered, and Jesus caught him. Entering the boat, they crossed over the lake to Gennesaret, where the inhabitants recognized Jesus and sent word all over the country that He was there. He healed the sick, even if they only touched Him.

So begins another day in the life of Jesus. How's that for hectic? With crowds pressing Him with their constant requests, no wonder Jesus sought solitary places *twice* in that busy day (Matthew 14:13, 23). Prayer gave Him the strength to meet the day's demands. If Jesus, the perfect Son of God, felt such an urgent need to get away and spend time with His Father, how much more should we feel that need? [4]

# BALANCING OUR PRAYERS

In John 17, Jesus prays a beautiful prayer for Himself, His followers at that time, and His followers to come. In this prayer, Jesus gives us another model. Jesus prays for Himself first, then for others. He spent about 20 percent of His prayer time for Himself and 80 percent for others.

We could pray in the same general ratio. We could, for example, divide our prayer time throughout the week to address different priorities:

| Day | Prayer Topic |
|---|---|
| Sunday | Church Requests |
| Monday | Self |
| Tuesday | Family |
| Wednesday | Church |
| Thursday | Work |
| Friday | World |
| Saturday | Special Requests |

The idea here is not to quantify our prayer life by a formula, but it might be helpful to give our prayers some balance in substance. Otherwise, we might find ourselves praying the same prayer every day and forgetting to mention something or someone important.

However, our prayers should not only focus on requests or supplication. Our prayers should not all be "gimme prayers." We also are taught to confess our sins, to be thankful, and to adore the greatness and goodness of God. These prayer elements form the mnemonic ACTS:

**A**doration (Psalm 9:1-2) – Praising God for what He is.

**C**onfession (1 John 1:9) – Asking God's forgiveness for our sins.

**T**hanksgiving (Colossians 4:2) – Thanking God for what He has done.

**S**upplication (Mark 11:24) – Asking God for what we need and want.

## THE PRAYER PRINCIPLES

Scripture has laid out for us certain principles that can help our prayers be more effective.

• Be persistent. Jesus told a parable about a widow who pestered a judge until he brought justice. Jesus made the analogy that if an ungodly judge responds to persistence, how much more will our heavenly Father bring justice to His chosen ones (Luke 18:1-6). "Pray continually" (1 Thessalonians 5:17).

• Be penitent. Jesus also told the story about a Pharisee and a tax collector who went to pray. The penitent tax collector was justified in his prayer, while the proud Pharisee was not (Luke 18:9-14).

• Be pardoning. "And when you stand praying, if you hold anything against anyone, forgive him, so that your Father in heaven may forgive you your sins" (Mark 11:25).

• Be plain-spoken. There is no need for flowery language or babbling on to God. He knows what we need before we ask (Matthew 6:7-8).

• Be private. Jesus often prayed alone in isolated places (Luke 5:16) and urged His followers to be private in their prayers (Matthew 6:5-6).

• Be praising. "Devote yourselves to prayer, being watchful and thankful" (Colossians 4:2).

• Be purposeful. While we want God to "bless everybody," the Bible gives us specific people for whom to pray, such as rulers (1 Timothy 2:1-4), the sick (James 5:15-16), and our enemies (Matthew 5:44).

## RENEWING OUR FRIENDSHIP

James 4:8 states, "Come near to God and He will come near to you." We can keep our relationship with our Father renewed when we listen to His Word and converse with Him frequently. In fact, He welcomes us to talk to Him all the time. (Find a friend who asks for that!) He longs for our constant company. He has made ample provision for communicating with us through His Word. He just wants to hear from us. Would any best friend ask for less?

# BALANCE CHECK

*Summarize John 15:12-17 in your own words.*

1. What are some different ways to study the Bible?
2. How can one memorize the Word?
3. Why is a mnemonic helpful in focusing our Bible study?
4. How can the Scriptures be beneficial to us (2 Timothy 3:15-17)?
5. How did Jesus exemplify a dynamic prayer life?
6. How can a Christian pray continually (1 Thessalonians 5:17; Luke 18:1; Ephesians 6:18; Philippians 4:6)?
7. What are some ways we can keep our prayers balanced?
8. What are some prayer principles taught in the Bible?
9. What did these people pray for, and how did God answer them? Who had regular prayer times?

    Elijah (1 Kings 18:36-38)

    Hezekiah (2 Kings 19:14-19, 35)

    Nehemiah (Nehemiah 2:4, 8)

    Daniel (Daniel 6:10, 23)

    Jonah (Jonah 2:1-2, 7, 10)

    Peter and John (Acts 4:24-29)

    Dorcas (Acts 9:40-41)

    Paul (2 Corinthians 12:7-10)

10. What did J. Hudson Taylor mean when he said, "Do not have your concert first and tune your instruments afterward. Begin the day with God"?

 # TIME OUT

*"A Bible that is falling apart probably belongs to someone who isn't."* – Christian Johnson [5]

*"God is not a cosmic bell-boy for whom we can press a button to get things."* – Harry Emerson Fosdick [6]

*"The Bible is God's chart for you to steer by, to keep you from the bottom of the sea, and to show you where the harbor is, and how to reach it without running on rocks or bars."* – Henry Ward Beecher [7]

*"I have been driven many times to my knees by the overwhelming conviction that I had nowhere else to go. My own wisdom, and that of all about me seemed insufficient for the day."* – Abraham Lincoln [8]

*"The Bible is a telescope; it is not to look at but to look through."* – Unknown [9]

*"Pray as if everything depended on God, and work as if everything depended on man."* – Francis Cardinal Spellman [10]

## CHAPTER 12

# RELATING TO YOUR RELATIVES

*"It's not what you have in your life, but who you have in your life that counts." – Unknown* [1]

Our world has changed from the idyllic days of family life in *Leave It to Beaver* and *Ozzie and Harriet*. Absent-father households, intergenerational stepfamilies, widespread divorce, and gay and lesbian households have expanded our culture's view of the traditional family. Families have problems, and they don't seem to be getting any better.

Relating to relatives is not just a problem of our generation; the Bible is full of disfunctional families. Sibling rivalry reached new heights with Joseph and his brothers. Mother-in-law Rebekah bemoaned her son's choice of wives, and Laban cheated his son-in-law Jacob. Adultery, incest, polygamy and rebellion were all a part of David's family life. Add to this childless parents (Abraham and Sarah initially), adopted children (Moses), interracial marriages (Moses and his Cushite wife), and stepfamilies (Solomon) and you have a real smorgasbord of relational issues. [2]

Whether in the past or the present, at its best the family can serve as a caring and nurturing atmosphere in which people can grow. Where else can we learn about what our relationship with God should be than in our families? Although our father/child relationship may be far from perfect on earth, we can better understand the ultimate relationship we long for with our heavenly Father.

## FAMILY FIRST?

Jesus knew the importance of family. When He healed the demon-possessed man, He told him to go home to his family to tell them what the Lord had done for him. Jesus knew that probably no one would be happier to hear his news than his family (Mark 5:19). He condemned the Jewish leaders for neglecting their parents as a pretense for giving to God (7:9-13). As He suffered excruciating pain on the cross, He remembered to ask John to care for His mother, Mary, who probably had been widowed (John 19:25-27).

But Jesus also knew that if there had to be a choice between Him and family, following Him would have to come first. In Luke 9:59-62, some men wanted to follow Jesus. One offered to follow Jesus after he buried his father. Probably his father was not dead, else he would already be home preparing for the funeral. He might not even have been old yet. But the man wanted to wait until his father was dead before he left home. Another man was ready to follow Jesus but first wanted to say goodbye to his family. In both cases, Jesus challenged them to stop stalling, leave their families and follow Him. [3]

In Luke 8:19-21, His mother and brothers sent Jesus a message that they wanted to see Him. He answered them by saying that spiritual bonds can be stronger than physical family bonds: "He replied, 'My mother and brothers are those who hear God's word and put it into practice' " (v. 21). Jesus knew His own family might not have fully understood His purpose because earlier they had tried to restrain Him when they thought He was out of his mind (Mark 3:21). He spoke of enemies being in one's own household and later added, "Anyone who loves his father or mother more than me is not worthy of me; and anyone who loves his son or daughter more than me is not worthy of me; and anyone who does not take his cross and follow me is not worthy of me" (Matthew 10:37).

This sacrifice is not without its benefits. Jesus repeats the necessary commitment in Matthew 19:29: "And everyone who has left houses or brothers or sisters or father or mother or children or fields for my sake will receive a hundred times as much and will inherit eternal life." The Christian's loss on earth is counterbalanced by the promise of heaven and blessings here, which include becoming members of the larger family of God. The commitment is worth it!

# KICKING THE CAT

We might be asked to decide between our families and God. We might not. God's Word makes it clear that if we do have to make a choice, He requires our full allegiance, but we often are called to give 110 percent to our families, which can leave us exhausted and short-changed. Soon we feel out of sorts and imbalanced.

Our homes are usually the first place to notice if we are out of balance. We might be kind to those outside the family, but when we are at home, we show our real selves by growling at the kids, ignoring our husbands, and kicking the cat. It's ironic that the ones we love the most sometimes see us at our worst. Our families usually know how we really feel.

Therefore, it is crucial for us to find the right balance in dealing with the people close to us. We must make time and effort to listen, hide a love note, read a story, play a game, bake cookies, make a phone call, send a letter, or take a trip because these people are special. We might have to give up some things in life, but these should not include our families. We might be replaced at the workplace, but no one can take our place in our families.

Sometimes things prevent us from giving our families the time and attention they need. Heavy work demands, extensive hobbies, active community work, unrealistic housekeeping expectations, even over-involvement in church activities – all these can take us away from our families and get our home lives out of kilter.

Let's look at some things that can help us keep our relationships in our families in balance so that we won't feel like kicking the cat!

### Be Flexible

The family is an ever-changing entity. Family members interact with others as they pass through different ages and stages. As soon as a child is born, he starts growing and changing. This transition will continue the rest of his life. It has been said not to worry too much about all these stages. By the time you have them figured out, another one will appear! So responding to these changes is a lifetime challenge.

Being flexible means being able to cope with these changes. For example, we understand that becoming a mother changes a woman's life. What happens after having three kids? With the first baby, you can't wait to shed your regular clothes and start wearing maternity clothes. By the third baby, your regular clothes *are* maternity clothes. With the first baby, you pore over baby name books and practice saying and writing combinations of your favorites. By the third baby, you close your eyes and point to a name in the book. With the first baby, you pick up your baby at the first sign of a whimper. By the third baby, you teach your toddler how to rewind the swing. With the first baby, you call home every half hour when you leave it with a sitter. By the third baby, you leave instructions only to call if there is blood. [4]

We must learn to adapt to changes in our ages, health, circumstances, jobs and financial situations. A child might have more problems than we think we can cope with. Death of a spouse or divorce can drastically affect our income and possibly even our work. Elderly parents might not be able to care for themselves. If we are flexible, like a well-rooted tree that gives with the storm, we will be more likely to withstand life's challenges. Michael McGriff said, "Blessed are the flexible, for they shall not be bent out of shape." [5] We have our God to lean on. "God is our refuge and strength, an ever-present help in trouble" (Psalm. 46:1).

### Communicate

Affluence has dealt a blow to communication in the family. For many families, things have become more important than people. With our frantic lifestyles, we don't make time to visit with each other anymore. According to an A.C. Nielson 1998 study, the average American, by the time she's 65, will have spent almost nine years glued to the television. We must find time to talk and listen again. [6]

Let's take advantage of the natural times when we can communicate with each other – shopping for groceries, working on household chores, riding in the car, conversing during mealtime.

Communication is enriched when it is one-to-one. Daily transition times – leaving for school, arriving home, and getting ready for bed – are opportune times to show concern about the day and shift gears. [7] Routines such as bedtime prayers offer a time to discuss events or problems of the day. Holiday traditions can provide meaningful opportunities to bring families together. Instead of everyone having separate hobbies, perhaps there could be some group hobbies like biking, camping or flying kites. One of the best times to be together is in family devotions and worship. [8]

### Delegate

Once a 4-year-old was looking at his parents' wedding pictures. He looked at his dad and asked, "Is this when Mommy came to work for us?"

In many families, the mother does the majority of the household chores, but she does not have to be enslaved by the "It's easier to do it by myself" syndrome.

One newlywed was determined her husband would learn how to carve their Thanksgiving turkey for their guests. As he eyed the turkey nervously, she whispered, "Go ahead and cut it like you learned in the book, dear."

"I learned all right," he answered. "But I don't see any of the dotted lines!" [9]

Family members can share in the responsibilities of running the house. A family meeting can determine what must be done regularly and how each person can help, based on time, ability or preference. List jobs and workers' names in a prominent place to eliminate excuses like "I forgot." Be willing to train children, and follow up on their performance. Praise their work if you can, make suggestions if needed, and then let them find their own way if the result is satisfactory. Some parents offer incentives like stickers on a chart for younger children and money or privileges for older ones. Perhaps an all-out effort for an hour on Saturday will foster a "we're all in this together" attitude. Taking part in the family teaches children responsibility and organizational skills, which will be valuable as they grow into adulthood. [10]

If you need more help than the family can provide, consider hir-

ing someone, even a high school or college student. In some cases, it is worth the money to have certain jobs done by someone
else. Don't forget technology that might make your life easier, especially in the kitchen. Decide if the job needs to be done at all or
if it can just be forgotten.

Whether a woman works inside or outside the home, many of
her hours are not her own. The Christian woman strives to be the
servant Jesus demonstrated when He washed the apostles' feet.
We should be willing to wash our families' feet, but they don't have
to walk all over us! There is a way to balance our work and time
so we can enjoy each other more.

## MAKING MEMORIES

Families are for building bridges and making memories. Our
children will remember the good memories, so we ought to make
as many as we can. They don't have to be expensive or planned.
Some of the greatest times are moments of serendipity.

Husband and wife should get away often and have fun. Dates
can be simple or elaborate, but too often they are given a low priority. Planned outings provide a good time to catch up on each other's life, make plans for the future, and just relax.

Remembering our extended families is also a good idea.
Reunions have achieved a new popularity. In some cases, these
times are the only ones when some relatives see each other.
Phone calls and e-mails are quick ways to keep in touch, while
videos of missed occasions are always appreciated.

We also need to have fun by ourselves. Whether for a walk in the
woods or a favorite movie, it is important to get away by ourselves.
When we have replenished our inner selves, we will be better
equipped to take care of those dearest to us.

"With the appearance of the two-bathroom home, Americans
forgot how to cooperate. With the appearance of the two-car family, we forgot how to associate, and with the coming of the two-
television home, we forgot how to communicate," writes John
Baucom. [11] We can't afford to forget any longer. Let's make relating to our relatives a priority again.

 BALANCE CHECK

*Summarize 1 Timothy 5:3-8 in your own words.*

1. How do we know that Jesus valued the family?

2. In Luke 9:59-62, what did the men want to do before they followed Jesus? How did Jesus answer them?

3. How did Jesus show that the Christian's commitment must be stronger to Him than to family (Matthew 10:37-38)?

4. What is our reward for such a commitment (Matthew 19:29)?

5. What can prevent us from giving our families the time and attention they need?

6. What are some changes that we must adapt to in growing families?

7. How does television prevent us from spending time with our families?

8. What are some natural times that we can communicate with our families?

9. What are some ways that families can share responsibilities in the running of the household?

10. What are some ways to spend more time with the family in work and in leisure?

 # TIME OUT

*"How many people on their deathbed wish they'd spent more time at the office?"* – Stephen Covey [12]

*"Light is the task when many share the toil."* – Homer [13]

*"A man who gives his children habits of industry provides for them better than by giving them a fortune."* – Richard Whatley [14]

*"The beauty of the home is order;*
*The blessing of the home is contentment*
*The glory of the home is hospitality;*
*The crown of the home is godliness."* – Unknown [15]

*"Is it relationships or dust-bunnies under your bed? Even when I've got a to-do list that would paper my living room, I sift through it quickly and decide what's important."* – Suzanne Frisse [16]

*"Why is it a woman is willing to share her whole life with her husband – but not her closet space?"* – Unknown [17]

## CHAPTER 13

# THEY'LL KNOW
# WE ARE CHRISTIANS

*"God never calls us to be ostriches."*
*– Miriam Adeny* [1]

Ira North, longtime preacher and author of the book *Balance: A Tried and Tested Formula for Church Growth*, tells of hearing a timid knock at the door of the the Madison Church of Christ building in Nashville. There he met two little girls aged about 10 and 8. The oldest one asked, "Mister, is this the church what helps people?"

He threw up his hands and exclaimed, "Well, I will declare. There are 750 churches in this town and you have found the right one. This is indeed the church what helps people." After hearing that their father was ill and out of work, Ira loaded them with groceries, invited them to Bible school, and showed them where their classes would be when they came. [2]

Wouldn't it be fantastic if every congregation of the Lord's church would be known as the "church what helps people"? So many people today are hungry physically – but even worse, they are starving spiritually. God designated us to meet their needs with the Bread and Water of Life. How are we meeting their needs? They are spiritually imbalanced and need to find the equilibrium of God's love. How well are we demonstrating that love?

Jesus told His followers how everyone would distinguish them from others: "By this all men will know that you are my disciples, if you love one another" (John 13:35). We should be known foremost by our love for each other. This love might be demonstrated in many different ways. But every action, every program, every plan should be motivated by love.

God knew that love is the great balancer of our lives. He knew that for all of us to get along, we need to level out our lives with love. How else could people of so many ages, temperaments, backgrounds and outlooks work together and reach out to others without tripping over their own problems? Someone has said, "Christians may not see eye-to-eye, but they can walk arm-in-arm." [3] Love is the glue that bonds us when we don't feel like sticking together. It is the ultimate element we must exhibit if we are to keep our balance.

## WAYS TO SHOW OUR LOVE

In striving to show our love, we can fall into three categories: those who make things happen, those who watch things happen; and those who wonder what happened! Which ones are we?

Paul exhorts us, "Therefore, as we have opportunity, let us do good to all people, especially to those who belong to the family of believers" (Galatians 6:10). In essence, Paul tells us that in caring for people to be sure we take care of God's family.

What part can we, as women, play in the church? Women are not to have authority over a man (1 Timothy 2:12), so we are limited in some aspects of the Lord's work. Instead of worrying about what we cannot do, let's get busy doing what we can! There are countless opportunities for all women, regardless of talent, age or health. Let's look at some of these opportunities.

• Pray! Some women meet regularly to pray about special needs.

• Prepare food for the bereaved, disaster victims, teacher appreciation dinners, elder and deacon appreciation dinners, men's breakfasts, fellowship potlucks and showers.

• Provide lodging for people attending gospel meetings, lectureships, singings and youth rallies.

• Plan retreats, ladies days, and mother/daughter banquets.

• Visit church members, sick, bereaved, needy and elderly.

• Send cards to the discouraged, sick and bereaved.

• Manage the church library or a clothing room or pantry for benevolence purposes.

• Organize a teacher's resource room.

• Attend Bible teacher workshops and gospel meetings.

• Teach Bible classes.

• Design Bible school curriculum.

• Prepare visuals for Bible teaching and bulletin boards.

• Paint and redecorate the church kitchen, classrooms and restrooms.

• Clean for the bereaved and sick.

• Transport the elderly and disabled.

• Support missionaries by writing them and sending tapes and packages.

• Type correspondence and church bulletin. [4]

It might not be possible for every congregation to plan every activity, but perhaps some might be rotated. For example, to avoid getting into a rut by doing the same thing every year, plan a women's retreat one year and a ladies day the next.

Not only can we find a balance in the church among different activities, but we also can balance our participation together. We can learn so much from each other by working together with ladies of various ages, spiritual maturity and marital status. By working together, we understand each other better and are better equipped to serve others outside the church.

## BEYOND OUR WALLS

Our challenge to find spiritual balance by loving begins with our brothers and sisters in Christ, but it doesn't end there. When we segregate ourselves entirely from the world, how can we ever reach them with the Good News? David Barrett said,

> Ninety-seven percent of all church ministries are directed toward Christians, rather than toward those outside of Christ, thus weakening Christianity's influence on the non-Christian world. [5]

The Barna Research Group reported that while 30 percent of the average church budget is allotted to building and maintenance, only five percent is spent on evangelism. [6] Often we become unbalanced when we spend more time, money and effort on works for church members to the neglect of those outside. We form a "holy huddle." Warren Bennis stated,

> Jesus said in the Great Commission that we should go into all the world (Matthew 28:19). Notice that he did not say we are to go into all the church. Are we in the church business or the world business? Are we in the institution business or the people business? [7]

Jesus literally rubbed elbows with the poor, the sick and the immoral. He said, "It is not the healthy who need a doctor, but the sick ... For I have not come to call the righteous, but sinners" (Matthew 9:12-13). But how do we usually act? While Jesus ate with the poor, the publicans and the sinners, we usually eat with our friends. He talked with outcasts; we avoid them. He found the sinner to try to lift him up. When we find the sinner, we often put him down.

Physically and spiritually, Jesus touched so many people in His ministry. Now that He has returned to the Father, He wants us to carry out His mission. Each one of us can reach a different person, perhaps someone our preachers or elders can't. We might be the only light that person will see. Let's make it count. There is so much women can do to spread God's love to an unloving world. Here are some ways:

• Sew clothing, quilts, lap robes for the poor, elderly and children's homes. Meeting together to work can make the job fun.

• Grade correspondence courses. These could be locally advertised with follow-up in the community or internationally promoted with missionary follow-up.

• Teach preschool and Mother's Day Out. Adults are often reached by their children's participation.

• Prepare food for Meals on Wheels, community and Thanksgiving dinners. Remember how Jesus said, "For I was hungry and you gave me something to eat, I was thirsty and you gave me something to drink" (Matthew 25:35).

• Pass out tracts. Include these with other church activities to the community, such as workshops and gospel meetings.

• Hold clothing giveaways. Maintain a clothing room by cleaning, updating and organizing clothing. Advertise your willingness to help.

• Welcome visitors, new babies and newcomers to the community. Some ladies deliver sunshine baskets full of helpful information about the community and church as well as simple gifts and New Testaments.

• Teach, write and visit women in prison. Bible classes could be held if allowed. Learn how other successful prison ministries are carried out.

• Vote for ethical and moral issues and pro-family candidates. Try to understand how issues affect our lives as Christians and where each candidate stands.

• Write, phone and e-mail political leaders, editors and companies concerning issues of moral concern. Speaking of writing media executives, Larry Poland said,

> By sheer numbers, if 70 million people who profess to be evangelical Christians would just write one letter a year that's gracious and to the point expressing their concern, 70 million letters would descend upon American media, and that would make a really significant difference, because they do read their mail. [8]

• Get involved in community affairs. Coach, run for office, serve on committees, volunteer in literacy programs or mentoring programs to make a difference and let your light shine.

• Stay informed. How can we serve the needs of others if we are uninformed. Miriam Adeny writes, "We have a responsibility to know what's happening in the world – to pray with the Bible in one hand and the newspaper in the other." [9]

Jesus compared His people to light on a hill (Matthew 5:14) and salt of the earth (v. 13). The real value of these elements comes, not when they are hidden away, but when they are distributed. We must spread God's love, not inhibit it to our worship assemblies and fellowship dinners.

What's the definition of real love? John tells us,

> This is how we know what love is: Jesus Christ laid down
> his life for us. And we ought to lay down our lives for
> our brothers. If anyone has material possessions and
> sees his brother in need but has no pity on him, how
> can the love of God be in him? Dear children, let us not
> love with words or tongue but with actions and in truth
> (1 John 3:16-18).

We can't do everything, but we can do something. Let's find the
something we can do and do it joyfully! We can't just lie down and
do nothing. As Adeney wrote, "We women perhaps are not raised
with a sufficient consciousness of battle. So we sunbathe while the
world burns." [10] Whether the world burns can depend on us and
our understanding of love.

## WRITING YOUR OWN LEGACY

Remember the woman who anointed Jesus? Jesus said that gen-
erations after her would hear of her act. The love we have shown
will not die when we die. It will live on in our works. Think how
Dorcas was remembered when she died. "All the widows stood
around him, crying and showing him the robes and other clothing that Dorcas had made while she was still with them." What a
tribute to a woman "who was always doing good and helping the
poor" (Acts 9:36). No wonder Peter was happy to raise such a faithful, kind woman from death to life. What an example for us!

How will you be remembered when you are gone? What will be
your legacy? Will the world know you for the love you demonstrated? Will your life have been balanced with actions and truth?

If your life could be summarized in a sentence, what would it
be? Would the engraving read, "She spent too much time watch-
ing television"? Or "She made a lot of money, but her children suffered for it"? How about, "Her life was so unbalanced, she never
got it together"?

Some epitaphs hit the truth quite poignantly, like this one in
New England: "She always made home happy." [11] Or this one from

New York: "She done her best." [12] Paul's summary of his life's work could serve as his epitaph: "I have fought the good fight, I have finished the race, I have kept the faith" (2 Timothy 4:7). Or how about Jesus' final statement on the cross, referring to His culmination of His life purpose: "It is finished" (John 19:30)?

Think about it – if you could plan your legacy, what would you want it to be? Would family and friends remember a life lived with godly balance? May God help us keep our balance as we build our legacies each day.

# BALANCE CHECK

*Summarize 1 John 3:16-20 in your own words.*

1. How did Jesus say the world would know who His disciples are (John 13:35)?
2. Why is it important to incorporate different groups, such as ages, marital status, and spiritual maturity, into the women's activities in the church?
3. Whom did Paul say we especially need to care for (Galatians 6:10)?
4. What are some ways to demonstrate our love in the church?
5. What are some ways to demonstrate our love in the world?
6. What are some ways to balance our activities to serve inside and outside the church?
7. Why is it important for a Christian to stay informed of world events?
8. What are some ways to get involved in your community to let your light shine?
9. How was Dorcas remembered when she died?
10. In what ways are Christians like salt and light?

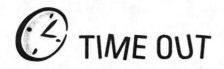 TIME OUT

*"Some people think the Great Commission is what the real estate agent gets when their house is sold."* – James R. Swanson [13]

*"A church should be an oasis of joy and hope in a desert of depression and fear."* – Brother Zorba [14]

*"The average church spends most of its resources, including money, man power, planning, activities, and services, on ... members and then wonders why it isn't growing, or catching any fish. They are not 'fishers of men'; they are keepers of the hatchery."* – John Hendee [15]

*"The life given us by nature is short: but the memory of a well-spent life is eternal."* – Cicero [16]

*"You can't make footprints in the sands of time sitting down."* – Unknown [17]

*"Don't be afraid your life will end; be afraid that it will never begin."* – Grace Hansen [18]

# ENDNOTES

**CHAPTER 1**
1. Peel, Kathy. *The Family Manager's Guide for Working Moms.* New York: Ballantine, 1997, p. 2.
2. Ibid., pp. 185-189.
3. Stautberg, Susan Schiffer and Marcia L. Worthing. *Balancing Acts! Juggling Work, Family, and Recreation.* New York: Master Media Limited, 1992, p. 3.
4. Young, Helen and Billie Silvey. *Time Management for Christian Women.* Grand Rapids, MI: Zondervan, 1990, p. 142.
5. Adams, Franklin P. ed. *FPA Book of Quotations.* New York: Funk & Wagnalls, 1952, p. 499.
6. http://www.ontonet.be/~smitsr/quotes/wisdom.html
7. Winokur, John. ed. *Friendly Advice.* New York: Plume, 1992, p. 106.
8. Hodgin, Michael. ed. *1001 More Humorous Illustrations for Public Speaking.* Grand Rapids, MI: Zondervan, 1998, p. 268.
9. Esar, Evan. ed. *Treasury of Humorous Quotations.* London: Phoenix House, 1951, p. 103.
10. "Happy New Year Blessing." Jan. 4, 1999, e-mail.

**CHAPTER 2**
1. Adams, Franklin P. ed. *FPA Book of Quotations.* New York: Funk & Wagnalls, 1952, p. 562.
2. Swenson, Richard. *Margin: How to Create the Emotional, Physical, Financial and Time Reserves You Need.* Colorado Springs: NavPress, 1992, pp.83-87.
3. *Reader's Digest Great Encyclopedic Dictionary.* Pleasantville, NY: Reader's Digest Association, 1966, p. 2022.
4. Babcock, Rachel. "Dare to Be Imperfect," *Christian Woman* Jan./Feb.1991, pp. 21-22.
5. Roper, Gayle G. *Balancing Your Emotions: For Women Who Want Consistency Under Stress.* Wheaton, IL: Harold Shaw Publishers, 1992, pp. 67-75.
6. Maggio, Rosalie. ed. *Impulse to Soar: Quotations for Women on Leadership.* Paramus, NJ: Prentice Hall, 1998, p. 194.
7. *Reader's Digest Great Encyclopedic Dictionary.* op. cit., p. 2043.
8. Peel, Kathy. *The Family Manager's Guide for Working Moms.* New York: Ballantine, 1997, p. 184.
9. Winokur, John. ed. *Friendly Advice.* New York: Plume, 1992, p. 139.
10. Flesch, Rudolf. ed. *The Book of Unusual Quotations.* New York: Harper & Brothers, 1957, p. 81.
11. Adams, op. cit., p. 561.

**CHAPTER 3**
1. Peter, Laurence J. *Peter's Quotations: Ideas for Our Time* (New York, Bantam, 1989), p. 306.
2. Smith, Alan. "Giving a Definite Maybe." Thought for the Day e-mail list, 11-4-98.

3. Davidson, Jeff. *The Complete Idiot's Guide to Managing Your Time.* New York: Alpha, 1998, p. 148.
4. Martin, Glen. *Beyond the Rat Race.* Nashville: Broadman & Holman, 1995, p. 27.
5. Ibid., pp. 58-61.
6. Comninellis, Nicholas. *Where Do I Go to Get a Life?.* Sisters, OR: Multnomah Books,1995, p. 125.
7. Roesch, Roberta. *The Working Woman's Guide to Managing Time.* Englewood Cliffs, NJ: Prentice Hall, 1996, p. 73.
8. Phillips, Bob. *Phillips' Book of Great Thoughts and Funny Sayings.* Wheaton, IL: Tyndale House, 1993, p. 170.
9. Ibid., p. 169.
10. Ibid., p. 88.
11. Ibid.
12. Zera, Richard S. ed. *1001 Quips and Quotes for Business Speeches.* New York: Sterling, 1992, p. 35.
13. Jones, Charlie T. and Bob Phillips. *Wit and Wisdom.* Eugene, OR: Harvest House, 1977, p. 25.

**CHAPTER 4**
1. Winokur, John. ed. *Friendly Advice.* New York: Plume, 1992, p. 140.
2. Covey, Stephen, A. Roger Merrill and Rebecca R. Merrill. *First Things First: To Live, to Love, to Learn, to Leave a Legacy.* New York: Fireside, 1995, pp. 88-89.
3. Lewis, Jack. *The Gospel According to Matthew, Part 2.* Abilene: ACU Press, 1984, p. 105.
4. Sherman, Doug and William Hendricks. *How to Balance Competing Time Demands: Keeping the Five Most Important Areas in Your Life in Perspective.* Colorado Springs: NavPress, 1989, pp. 51-53.
5. Ibid., p. 83.
6. Comninellis, Nicholas. *Where Do I Go to Get a Life?.* Sisters, OR: Multnomah Books,1995, p. 154.
7. *God's Little Instruction Book for Graduates.* Tulsa: Honor Books, 1994, p. 61.
8. Hummel, Charles. *Priorities – Tyranny of the Urgent: Six Studies for Individuals or Groups.* Leicester, NY: InterVarsity, 1994, p. 6.
9. Buckner, Jeannie. "Time Management for the Family – Part II." *Focus Issue: Marriage and Family Development.* Minneapolis: Family Information Services, Nov. 1997, pp. 65-66.
10. Comninellis, op. cit, p. 154.
11. Sherman and Hendricks, op. cit., p. 83.
12. Peel, Kathy. *The Family Manager's Guide for Working Moms.* New York: Ballantine Books, 1997, p. 49.
13. Ibid., p.11.
14. Ibid., p. 30.
15. Ibid., p. 37.

16. Green's Lake Road Church of Christ bulletin. East Ridge, Tenn., Aug. 8, 1999, p. 3.
17. Ashcroft, Mary Ellen. *Balancing Act: How Women Can Lose Their Roles and Find Their Calling.* Downers Grove, IL: InterVarsity Press, 1996, p. 159.

**CHAPTER 5**
1. Gregory, Susan. *Out of the Rat Race: A Practical Guide to Taking Control of Your Time and Money So You Can Enjoy Life More.* Ann Arbor, MI: Vine Books, 1994, p. 13.
2. Byalick, Marcia and Linda Saslow. *The Three-Career Couple: Mastering the Art of Juggling Work, Home and Family.* Princeton, NJ: Peterson's, 1993, pp. 16-17.
3. http://tftd.faithsite.com/content.asp?CID=27036
4. Sherman, Doug and William Hendricks. *How to Balance Competing Time Demands: Keeping the Five Most Important Areas in Your Life in Perspective.* Colorado Springs: NavPress, 1989, pp. 130-132.
5. Young, Helen and Billie Silvey. *Time Management for Christian Women.* Grand Rapids, MI: Zondervan, 1990, pp. 39-40.
6. Buckner, Jeannie. "Time Management for the Family – Part II," *Focus Issue: Marriage and Family Development.* Minneapolis: Family Information Services, Nov. 1997, p. 63.
7. Hughey, Billy and Janice Hughey. *A Rainbow of Hope.* El Reno, OK: Rainbow Studies, 1994, p. 62.
8. Wellwood, Jackie. *The Busy Mom's Guide to Simple Living.* Wheaton, IL: Crossway Books, 1997, pp. 144-145.
9. Peter, Laurence J. *Peter's Quotations: Ideas for Our Time.* New York: Bantam, 1989, p. 305.
10. Phillips, Bob. *Phillips' Book of Great Thoughts and Funny Sayings.* Wheaton, IL: Tyndale House, 1993, p. 26.
11. Adams, Franklin P. ed. *FPA Book of Quotations.* New York: Funk & Wagnalls, 1952, p. 631.
12. Zera, Richard S. ed. *1001 Quips and Quotes for Business Speeches.* New York: Sterling Publishing, 1992, p. 106.
13. Phillips, op. cit., p. 142.
14. Campbell, David. *If You Don't Know Where You're Going, You'll Probably End Up Somewhere Else.* Niles, IL: Argus Communications, 1974, p. 13.

**CHAPTER 6**
1. Martin, Glen. *Beyond the Rat Race.* Nashville: Broadman & Holman, 1995, p. 93.
2. Littleton, Mark. *Escaping the Time Crunch.* Chicago: Moody Press, 1990, p. 105.
3. Porat, Frieda. *Creative Procrastination: Organizing Your Own Life.* San Francisco: Harper & Row, 1980, p. 82.
4. Ibid., p. 88.

5. Buckner, Jeannie. "Organizational Skills for the Family." *Focus Issue: Marriage and Family Development.* Minneapolis: Family Information Services, May 1998, pp. 20-21.

6. Peel, Kathy. *The Family Manager's Guide for Working Moms.* New York: Ballantine, 1997, p. 67.

7. Walker, Deward E. ed. *Handbook of North American Indians, Plateau,* V.12. Washington, D.C.: U.S. Government Printing Office, 1998, p. 337.

8. Peel, op. cit., p. 66.

9. "Something to Think About," SISTERS e-mail list, June 22, 1998.

10. Phillips, Bob. *Phillips' Book of Great Thoughts and Funny Sayings.* Wheaton, IL: Tyndale House, 1993, p. 311.

11. Hughey, Billy and Janice Hughey. *A Rainbow of Hope.* El Reno, OK: Rainbow Studies, 1994, p. 74.

12. Peter, Laurence J. *Peter's Quotations: Ideas for Our Time.* New York: Bantam, 1989, p. 497.

13. Griessman, B. Eugene. *Time Tactics of Very Successful People.* New York: McGraw-Hill, 1994, p. xiii.

14. Adams, Franklin P. ed. *FPA Book of Quotations.* New York: Funk & Wagnalls, 1952, p. 556.

15. Ibid., p. 791.

## CHAPTER 7

1. Lynberg, Michael. *The Path with Heart.* New York: Fawcett Columbine, 1990, p. 40.

2. Johnson, Eric. *A Treasury of Humor: An Indexed Collection of Anecdotes.* Buffalo: Prometheus, 1989, p. 185.

3. Friedman, Edward L. *Toastmaster's Treasury.* New York: Harper & Row, 1960, p. 255.

4. Schor, Juliet. *The Overworked American: The Unexpected Decline of Leisure.* New York: Basic, 1991, p. 107.

5. Ibid., p. 109.

6. Ibid., p. 3.

7. Phillips, Bob. *Phillips' Book of Great Thoughts and Funny Sayings.* Wheaton, IL: Tyndale House, 1993, p. 186.

8. Lynberg, op. cit., p. 40.

9. Powell, Terry. *Balanced Living on a Tightrope.* Wheaton, Ill.: Victor, 1991, p. 100.

10. Comninellis, Nicholas. *Where Do I Go to Get a Life?.* Sisters, OR: Multnomah Books, 1995, p. 77.

11. Barclay, William. *The Gospel of Luke.* Philadelphia: Westminster Press, 1973, pp. 207-210.

12. Swenson, Richard. *Margin: How to Create the Emotional, Physical, Financial and Time Reserves You Need.* Colorado Springs: NavPress, 1992, p. 179.

13. Ibid., pp. 168-169.

14. Winokur, John. ed. *Friendly Advice.* New York: Plume, 1992, p. 165.

15. Ramsey, Dave. *Financial Peace.* New York: Viking, 1995, p. 29.

16. Mead, Frank. ed. *Encyclopedia of Religious Quotations*. Westwood, NJ: Revell, 1965, p. 310.
17. Ibid., p. 309.
18. Jones, Charlie T. and Bob Phillips. *Wit and Wisdom*. Eugene, OR: Harvest House, 1977, p. 99.
19. Flesch, Rudolf. ed. *The Book of Unusual Quotations*. New York: Harper & Brothers, 1957, p. 178.
20. *Reader's Digest Great Encyclopedic Dictionary*. Pleasantville, NY: Reader's Digest Association, 1966, p. 2030.
21. Peter, Laurence J. *Peter's Quotations: Ideas for Our Time*. New York: Bantam, 1989, p. 346.

**CHAPTER 8**
1. Peel, Kathy. *The Family Manager's Guide for Working Moms*. New York: Ballantine, 1997, p. 51.
2. Author unknown, e-mail.
3. Swenson, Richard. *Margin: How to Create the Emotional, Physical, Financial and Time Reserves You Need*. Colorado Springs: NavPress, 1992, p.199.
4. Schofield, Deniece. *Confessions of an Organized Housewife*. Cincinnati: Writer's Digest Books, 1982, p. 58.
5. Barnes, Emilie. *Emilie's Creative Home Organizer*. Eugene, OR: Harvest House, 1995, p. 184.
6. "Point of View." SISTERS e-mail list, May 13, 1999.
7. *God's Little Instruction Book for Graduates*. Tulsa: Honor Books, 1994, p. 35.
8. Esar, Evan. ed. *Treasury of Humorous Quotations*. London: Phoenix House, 1951, p. 80.
9. Ibid., p. 157.
10. Phillips, Bob. *Phillips' Book of Great Thoughts and Funny Sayings*. Wheaton, IL: Tyndale House, 1993, p. 248.
11. Adams, Franklin P. ed. *FPA Book of Quotations*. New York: Funk & Wagnalls, 1952, p. 195.
12. Ibid., p. 639.

**CHAPTER 9**
1. Adeney, Miriam. *A Time for Risking: Priorities for Women*. Portland, OR: Multnomah Press, 1987, p. 27.
2. Shipp, Glover and Kent Markum. " 'Mama Lou' Smiddy, Oldest Missionary, Dies in Ecuador at 103." *Christian Chronicle* February 1999, p. 36.
3. Zera, Richard S. ed. *1001 Quips and Quotes for Business Speeches*. New York: Sterling Publishing, 1992, p. 59.
4. Ibid., p. 80.
5. Hughey, Billy and Janice Hughey. *A Rainbow of Hope*. El Reno, OK: Rainbow Studies, 1994, p. 63.

6. Johnson, Nancy Lavender. "Ministry of Quiet Service." *Christian Woman* Sept./Oct. 1997, pp. 16-18.
7. Adeney, op. cit., pp. 8, 23-24.
8. Hughey and Hughey, op. cit., p. 147.
9. Turner, Denise. *Scuff Marks on the Ceiling.* Waco, TX: Word Books, 1986, p. 149.
10. Zera, op. cit., p. 42.
11. Ibid.
12. Adams, Franklin P. ed. *FPA Book of Quotations.* New York: Funk & Wagnalls, 1952, p. 2.
13. Phillips, Bob. *Phillips' Book of Great Thoughts and Funny Sayings.* Wheaton, IL: Tyndale House, 1993, p. 58.
14. Ibid., p. 59.
15. Esar, Evan. ed. *Treasury of Humorous Quotations.* London: Phoenix House, 1951, p. 194.

**CHAPTER 10**

1. Simpson, James B. *Contemporary Quotations.* New York: Thomas Y. Crowell, 1964, p. 251.
2. *Reader's Digest Great Encyclopedic Dictionary.* Pleasantville, NY: Reader's Digest Association, 1966, p. 2053.
3. Ibid., p. 2041.
4. Davidson, Jeff. *The Complete Idiot's Guide to Managing Your Time.* New York: Alpha, 1998, p. 190.
5. Griessman, B. Eugene. *Time Tactics of Very Successful People.* New York: McGraw-Hill, 1994, p. 66.
6. Swenson, Richard. *Margin: How to Create the Emotional, Physical, Financial and Time Reserves You Need.* Colorado Springs: NavPress, 1992, p. 115.
7. Martin, Glen. *Beyond the Rat Race.* Nashville: Broadman & Holman, 1995, p. 134.
8. Schor, Juliet. *The Overworked American: The Unexpected Decline of Leisure.* New York: Basic, 1991, pp. 11, 20.
9. Lunden, Joan and Laura Morton. *Joan Lunden's Healthy Living: A Practical, Inspirational Guide to Creating Balance in Your Life.* New York: Crown, 1997, p. 235.
10. Keyes, Ralph. "How to Unlock Time." *Reader's Digest* Oct. 1991, pp. 112-113.
11. Mead, Frank. ed. *Encyclopedia of Religious Quotations.* Westwood, NJ: Revell, 1965, p. 212.
12. Peel, Kathy. *The Family Manager's Guide for Working Moms.* New York: Ballantine, 1997, p. 194.
13. Adams, Franklin P. ed. *FPA Book of Quotations.* New York: Funk & Wagnalls, 1952, p. 416.
14. Ibid., p. 492.
15. Esar, Evan. ed. *Treasury of Humorous Quotations.* London: Phoenix House, 1951, p. 187.

16. Bradley, John P., Leo F. Daniels and Thomas C. Jones. eds. *International Dictionary of Thoughts.* Chicago: J. G. Ferguson, 1969, p. 90.
17. Samra, Cal and Rose Samra. *More Holy Humor.* Nashville: Thomas Nelson, 1997), p. 166.

**CHAPTER 11**
1. Esar, Evan. ed. *Treasury of Humorous Quotations.* London: Phoenix House, 1951, p. 162.
2. Martin, Glen. *Beyond the Rat Race.* Nashville: Broadman & Holman, 1995, p. 88.
3. Fleming, Jean. *Between Walden and the Whirlwind: Living the Christ-Centered Life.* Colorado Springs: NavPress, 1985, p. 65.
4. Flatt, Steve. *In Jesus Name.* Madison, TN: Christian Productions, 1991. Video.
5. Samra, Cal and Rose Samra. *More Holy Humor.* Nashville: Thomas Nelson, 1997), p. 139.
6. Adams, Franklin P. ed. *FPA Book of Quotations.* New York: Funk & Wagnalls, 1952, p. 646.
7. Phillips, Bob. *Phillips' Book of Great Thoughts and Funny Sayings.* Wheaton, IL: Tyndale House, 1993, p. 43.
8. Ibid., p. 247.
9. Zera, Richard S. ed. *1001 Quips and Quotes for Business Speeches.* New York: Sterling, 1992, p. 157.
10. Ibid., p. 157.

**CHAPTER 12**
1. Unknown source.
2. Gangel, Kenneth O. and James C. Wilhoit, *The Christian Educator's Handbook in Family Life Education.* Grand Rapids, MI: Baker Books, 1996, pp. 36-68.
3. Barclay, William. *The Gospel of Luke.* Philadelphia: Westminster, 1973, pp. 131-132.
4. *"Humor – Things My Mother Taught Me."* SISTERS e-mail list, Dec. 3, 1998.
5. Hughey, Billy and Janice Hughey. *A Rainbow of Hope.* El Reno, OK: Rainbow Studies, 1994, p. 168.
6. Eyre, Richard and Linda Eyre. *Lifebalance.* New York: Ballantine, 1988, p. 236.
7. http://www.tvfa.org
8. Alden, Ada. "Books That Inspire ... The Intentional Family." *Focus Issue: Marriage and Family Development.* Minneapolis: Family Information Services, November 1998, pp. 45, 47.
9. Droke, Maxwell. *The Speaker's Handbook of Humor.* New York: Harper & Row, 1956, p. 159.
10. Alden, op. cit., p. 45.

11. Peel, Kathy. *The Family Manager's Guide for Working Moms.* New York: Ballantine, 1997, p. 51.
12. Covey, Stephen, A. Roger Merrill and Rebecca R. Merrill. *First Things First: To Live, To Love, To Learn, To Leave a Legacy.* New York: Fireside, 1995, p. 17.
13. Adams, Franklin P. ed. *FPA Book of Quotations.* New York: Funk & Wagnalls, 1952, p. 867.
14. Phillips, Bob. *Phillips' Book of Great Thoughts and Funny Sayings.* Wheaton, IL: Tyndale House, 1993, p. 171.
15. Adams, op. cit., p. 432.
16. Roesch, Roberta. *The Working Woman's Guide to Managing Time.* Englewood Cliffs, NJ: Prentice Hall, 1996, p. 211.
17. Jones, Charlie T. and Bob Phillips. *Wit and Wisdom.* Eugene, OR: Harvest House, 1977, p. 128.

**CHAPTER 13**
1. Adeney, Miriam. *A Time for Risking: Priorities for Women.* Portland, OR: Multnomah Press, 1987, p. 43.
2. North, Ira. *Balance: A Tried and Tested Formula for Church Growth.* Nashville: Gospel Advocate Co., 1983, pp. 55-56.
3. Mead, Frank. ed. *Encyclopedia of Religious Quotations.* Westwood, NJ: Revell, 1965, p. 37.
4. Mills, Jo Ann. "Service in an Organized Manner." *Christian Woman* July/Aug. 1998, pp. 48-51.
5. "Excerpts." *Christian Chronicle* Dec. 1998, p. 23.
6. Hendee, John. *Smart Fishing: Ways a Congregation Can Reach More People for Christ.* Cincinnati: Standard, 1991, p. 11.
7. Ibid., p. 28.
8. Neven, Tom. "Salt and Light in Hollywood." *Focus on the Family* Dec. 1998, pp. 10-11.
9. Adeney, op. cit., p. 105.
10. Ibid., p. 142.
11. Pike, Richard. ed. *Remarkable Blunders, Advertisements and Epitaphs.* London: John Heywood, 19–, p. 154.
12. Beable, W. H., ed. *Epitaphs: Graveyard Humour and Eulogy.* New York: Thomas Y. Crowell, 1925, p. 17
13. Samra, Cal and Rose Samra. *More Holy Humor.* Nashville: Thomas Nelson, 1997, p. 144.
14. Ibid., p. 180.
15. Hendee, op. cit., pp. 10-11.
16. Adams, Franklin P. ed. *FPA Book of Quotations.* New York: Funk & Wagnalls, 1952, p. 503.
17. Phillips, Bob. *Phillips' Book of Great Thoughts and Funny Sayings.* Wheaton, IL: Tyndale House, 1993, p. 311.
18. Winokur, John. ed. *Friendly Advice.* New York: Plume, 1992, p. 147.

CPSIA information can be obtained at www.ICGtesting.com
Printed in the USA
LVOW13s1532081213

364378LV00002B/2/A